THE HOUR OF THE LOCUST

Yang Zhengguang was born in Qian County, Shaanxi, in 1957. After graduating from Shandong University in 1982 with a degree in Chinese literature, he moved to the city of Tianjin to be part of the Chinese People's Political Consultative Conference, an advisory body promoting multi-party cooperation. Four years later, he moved to a small village in northern Shaanxi to write poetry.

He then became a successful scriptwriter, most notably adapting the classic Chinese epic *The Outlaws of the Marsh* to great acclaim. Yang also founded and served as CEO of the Chang'an Film & Television Production Company, and became chairman of the Shenzhen Association of Literature and Art.

This book is part of Shaanxi Stories, a series of translated works by acclaimed authors from the Shaanxi province of China, produced by Valley Press in collaboration with Northwest University, Xi'an. The series editors are Hu Zongfeng and Robin Gilbank. Other books in the series:

MOUNTAIN STORIES, Ye Guangqin
HOW OLD DAN BECAME A TREE, Yang Zhengguang
THE EARTHEN GATE, Jia Pingwa
THE BLOOD RED SUN, Wu Keijing
THE HOWL OF THE WOLF, Hong Ke
THE WILD LAND, Jia Pingwa
IRRATIONAL THINGS, Mu Tao
SUN PALACE, Ye Guangqin

The Hour of the Locust

Yang Zhengguang

*translated by He Longping
and Robin Gilbank*

Valley Press

First published in 2021 by Valley Press
Woodend, The Crescent, Scarborough, YO11 2PW
www.valleypressuk.com

ISBN 978-1-912436-79-8
Cat. no. VP0196

Copyright © Yang Zhengguang 2021

The right of Yang Zhengguang to be identified as the
author of this work has been asserted in accordance with
the Copyright, Designs and Patents Act 1988.

All rights reserved. No part of this publication may be
reproduced, stored in or introduced into a retrieval system,
or transmitted in any form, by any means (electronic,
mechanical, photocopying, recording or otherwise) without
prior written permission from the rights holders.

A CIP record for this book is available from the British Library.

Text and cover design by Peter Barnfather.
Cover art: *'Ah, you little thief!' said the farmer in
an angry voice.* (1925) by Attilio Mussino.
Series edited by He Longping and Robin Gilbank.

Printed and bound in Great Britain
by Clays Ltd, Elcograf S.p.A.

I.

The locusts descended with a howl. Nobody instructed them to swarm; they came without warning and no omen prophesied their arrival. The howl was akin to an iron shovelful of dirt being flung heavenward, and they soared into the western skies as though a demon was driving them to blot out the sun.

The villagers tending their crops in the fields were the first to catch sight of the threat. The neat, thriving rows of maize stalks had already reached half the height of a man and the growers had not counted on the appearance of a plague such as this. They stood up to scan the sky in the belief that a whirlwind was whipping up or a sandstorm was in the offing. However, something was amiss – the sound was wrong. A whirlwind or a sandstorm only whistles. There is never the pulsating strain of *ge zha zha, ge zha zha* added into the mix.

The rhythm unnerved them. Their faces dropped and after letting out a short sharp yelp, they loosened their legs to hotfoot it back to their village.

They didn't know why the noise of the locusts filled them with dread.

Later, they drew a sober comparison between the locusts and a whirlwind or a sandstorm. A whirlwind was indeed frightening but did not chill you to the marrow as the locusts did. A whirlwind spins and spins and might be capable of skirting around roadblocks. If it fails to negotiate these obstacles, trees and houses will be uprooted and people sent hurtling into the air. When these poor sods are splattered down onto the ground, they are dead meat; senseless and with no concept of fear. What about a sandstorm? In this case, people simply need to scrunch their eyes closed and clamp their hands over their nostrils before leaving themselves to its merciless wiles. After the storm has passed, nothing more grievous will be left behind than a coating of dust. Is that really such a bane?

But those donkey-fucked bastards – the locusts – were neither whirlwinds nor sandstorms. They not only whistled like a demented wind but also pulsated with a *ge zha zha, ge zha zha*. It was truly exasperating.

Weren't these creatures just the same as common-or-garden grasshoppers, apt to hop a few times and hover for a while? They were neither brave nor gregarious. How could they have been transformed into a gargantuan swarm? How could they whistle overhead like a demented wind with that eerie tone until the skies were blotted out and the sun was eclipsed?

The villagers heard tell later that a portion of a locust's hind legs ought never to be touched. Doing so stimulates it most violently and, once stimulated in that way, its natural disposition alters. The creatures are now inclined to congregate. Not only do they congregate but they migrate collectively. They can fly for three whole days and nights without landing and, wherever they eventually descend, catastrophe ensues.

Which idle donkey-fucked prick pushed his luck by tugging a critter's leg? If they had to take wing, they should have kept flying and flying. Couldn't they just have flown themselves to death? It beggared belief.

All the villagers slunk out from their compounds or courtyards onto the street. With stiffened necks and nervous pupils, they surveyed the western skies until their eyes were reduced to two hollows, and then in chorus they let out a cry.

They did that only once. Everyone was able to expel a single cry before the locusts cascaded down on their heads. Seized with shock, they couldn't muster another. Their hearts contracted into fleshy lumps and their throats squeezed tight, leaving not even the tiniest crack through which a whisper could be released. In frightening situations, being able to shriek several times can usually induce mild catharsis. The villagers were only given the chance to do it once.

Their voices were rendered inaudible by the din. The locusts had not only blotted out the sun and slathered the skies, but their insane wind-like whistling and *ge zha zha, ge zha zha* noise readied them to churn the heavens and turn the earth upside down. Though all the villagers lined up in chorus to cry out together under the direction of a conductor, they still couldn't be heard – they could never out-cry the locusts.

They galloped back to their respective homes with their hands wrapped about their heads and slammed the doors shut.

Why did they wrap their hands around their heads? The locusts were not airborne brickbats. Even if the locusts had been brickbats, they were not aimed specifically at them.

Why did they shut their doors tight after running back home? They placed too much faith in their rooms, believing they would be kept safe as long as they shut themselves in. A room is used to keep out wind and rain, to block the ogling eyes of neighbours and, of course, to parry the brickbats flung by a foe. But the locusts could be counted as neither wind nor rain. They didn't mean to pry in their private affairs. There was no feud or standing grudge between them. They didn't need to change themselves into brickbats to settle a score and disperse rancour. Locusts were locusts. They had no interest in folks' heads and no interest in folks' homes. They were interested only in the crops in their fields, or, to be precise, they were greedy for the maize stalks that were already half the height of a grown man.

The mad wind-like whistling died down so that only the *ge zha zha, ge zha zha* drone remained. They knew that the locusts had landed and were gnawing away and munching on their produce. In every compound, villagers sat up straight as crossbow bolts, listening carefully and waiting patiently for three days and three nights.

There were some impatient listeners among them; listeners who didn't want to take the situation lying down. They were only locusts when all was said and done. "We are people!" the villagers reasoned. "Should we just keep quiet and let the vermin screw us over like this?" Those who were so minded threw their doors open and ran out from the community. They saw how the locusts were gnawing and chewing their crops. There were far, far too many of them, beyond the everyday notion of number in fact. While emitting a pulsating noise, they spread out in a tightly-knit configuration across the fields, which stretched as far as who-knows-where. How conscientiously they gnawed and munched. How meticulously, how leisurely and how methodically. Weren't the maize stalks already half the height of a man? They stood on top of each other like they were erecting scaffolding and devoured from the top down to the base. After they had razed one patch, they would move onto the neighbouring plot of farmland and continue masticating.

Kick those donkey-fucked bastards! Do you think your feet are equal to the challenge? You couldn't kick them away even if you wore your feet into broken stumps.

Squash those donkey-fucked bastards! One well-placed stomp would create a pest pancake. But feet and legs have finite strength. How many locusts could you hope to squash? Inevitably, you would end up sitting down hard, feeling dog-tired from having stamped so much, and would be left staring at them gnawing and munching while making that eerie noise.

Yet, if you were to think about this dispassionately, you had to admire the locusts. After three days and nights, they suddenly disappeared without informing the villagers and without leaving any clues. They went as they had arrived. None of the locals saw them go.

Not only the maize stalks had been demolished but all kinds of grasses and tree leaves too; not a speck could now be detected in boundless square miles. All the land had assumed a uniform hue and had become a single expanse, bald, denuded and sun-beaten. Like the victims of highway robbers left without a stitch to wear, the naked land told onlookers: "Stop staring. There is nothing to gawp at. They've done a thorough job."

Meanwhile, the villagers asked: "Donkey-fucked bastards, why didn't you lay waste to us rather than our crops? Why did you let us live yet do us out of our livelihood?"

"Is this what they call a natural disaster? You have disaster thrust upon you and get screwed over despite there being no feud or hatred to speak of."

"You're really talking about a heaven-sent disaster. Must you call it a natural disaster? I expect you want to sound educated."

"No, no, no. A whirlwind or a sandstorm is a natural disaster. So too is an earthquake. So was the worst drought in the first half of this year. But we are talking about locusts."

"That's what's called a pest disaster!"

It was not uncommon to see folk gather in the village to grind their idle teeth like this. In fact, they did have food rations during the few days that followed. It was untrue to say that nothing had been left behind after the locusts flew away. Once they took wing, many dead bodies littered the ground. The pest pancakes were the handiwork of stamping feet. Still more lay crushed on the ground. No one could work out how they died. Did they trample each other to death when they were chewing in a tight scrum? Or did they press each other to death while they were raising their scaffolding to strip the maize stalks from the top to the base? Or did they simply gorge themselves to death? They kept on gorging for three consecutive days and nights. Wouldn't some bloat themselves to their doom? Nobody really investigated this problem. The dead bodies were left behind and became people's food rations. With some villagers toting woven grass creels and some carrying baskets on their backs, they scrambled to sweep up as many corpses as they could. A few even made use of the hessian sacks that were originally used to hoard grain. After these were filled, they were shaken for a while and then pressed down a little so that more could be forced in. The sacks were finally all packed solid. During the process of scrambling, there were those who bickered or even hurled abuse until they were ready to throw punches and kicks. Luckily, the number of dead locusts was finite, and they were snapped up in no time.

How could they be made into meals? The locusts were rather plump. Their bodies were fleshy and greasy. After being stir-fried in a wok, they became crunchy and had a kind of savoury smell. In the following few days, the villagers had a taste of the good life. Nonetheless, soon afterwards the downside became evident – many folks couldn't evacuate their bowels and had to resort to gouging out what was left behind with their fingers. All they were able to prod free were locust shells.

Until then, it had not occurred to anybody that dead locusts might be utilised as food rations. Still, they were hardly food rations in the true meaning of the term. The locusts that filled their bowls had munched into ruins the road that once led to their true sustenance.

The villagers habitually cultivated two harvests a year. Their crops in the first half of the year had all perished owing to a terrible drought and the stalks were only fit for firewood. Failing to yield even one edible grain, the farmland bared its teeth and twisted its mouth as if to protest. The villagers too bared their teeth and contorted their mouths. With twisted expressions, they smoothed the distorted face of the fields and dug it to a tilth using brute force and sweat. They planted the second round of crops. They gazed at them longingly as they reached half the height of a man. With a *whoosh*, the locusts flooded down.

"Donkey-fucked bastards! It would have been OK if you'd left it until next year to come. If you'd let us bring home one round of crops and lay our hands on some food rations, we could have scraped by. Why did you have to pick this of all times to come? *Ai! Ai!*"

"It was the drought that caused those donkey-fucked bastards to knock their hind legs against one another's. They ganged up together to fly blindly."

Whenever he heard conversations like this, fifty-nine-year-old Profound Meditation Wu would fling the same five words at those who were speaking with a disdainful look: "You're yanking at your balls." A number of villagers had already starved to death. Many had deserted their compounds and courtyards to flee the famine, pushing a handcart or carrying a load on their shoulders. Profound Meditation Wu thought such exchanges beneath contempt. In his eyes, talking like this in such a critical situation was worse than chatting idly or being stubborn-tongued. It simply amounted to yanking at their balls – there was movement but no real action.

After that, a donkey-back gang was raised.

2.

A donkey-back gang was, it must be said, a simpler entity than a swarm of locusts.

A voice cut through the air: "We can't go on yanking at our balls. Our stomachs are grumbling. We could run away from our starving home village, we could go to a faraway place to beg, or we could sprout a third hand and become a thief…"

"Never. We should swing into action and never resort to cheap shots."

This was another thought thrown out by Profound Meditation Wu. In a grass shelter outside the village, a dozen people – old, middle-aged and young – put their heads together. They hadn't yet left their village. They all wanted to do something, though no one knew how to go about it, and so simply huddled together to thrash out a plan. All of them agreed with Profound Meditation Wu's opinion that they should "swing into action and never resort to cheap shots".

Profound Meditation Wu was the oldest among them and the only one who had not turned bitter under the torment of starvation. He was tall, withered and bony like a stalk of hemp. He had thievishly small eyes that glistened like those of a rat. In his thirties, he married a woman who succumbed to a disease before she could bear him a son or daughter. He had remained single ever since but was conducting an assignation with a widow in the village; every three to five days he would head to the widow's *kang* for a spot of relaxation. She was among those who had bolted to escape the famine. He didn't try to persuade her to stay nor did he follow her. He was unwilling to flee from his stricken homeland because he wanted to be true to his word: never resort to cheap shots.

Now, planting himself among his fellow villagers, Profound Meditation Wu didn't allow his small eyes to blink – which they would only do when he was feverish with excitement. He proceeded to deliver a speech to the eleven others crouching or sitting on the floor. "We should never seek refuge with our relatives or friends," he harangued. "We should never reach out a hand to beg, and we should never be a ruffian with three hands. But at the same time, we should not sit on our hands waiting to starve."

"Don't mention the word *starve*," Earthen Jar interrupted him. "It reminds me of when I stuffed myself on dead locusts to survive and then couldn't crap. Now even the stuff that blocks your guts has all been eaten up. But still you go on about being *starved*!"

Earthen Jar was not his original name. It was a nickname given on account of how his head was shaped like a terracotta pot. Earthen Jar was pained in both his facial expressions and intonation. He didn't want Profound Meditation Wu to slip the word *starve* into his speech. He was the youngest one among the dozen.

Profound Meditation Wu didn't show even a scrap of sympathy. "Yanking at your balls."

Feeling irritated, Earthen Jar stood up. "No, my hand is on my arse cheeks. Can't you see that?"

Earthen Jar turned his rear end towards Profound Meditation Wu. His hand really was glued to his posterior. Earthen Jar explained that he had poked away at his bunghole too much and it had not healed up entirely.

"You're yanking at your balls," was Wu's refrain.

Earthen Jar squatted down. "OK, I was yanking at my balls just now."

Profound Meditation picked up where he left off. "A man can't do a thing about the Old Lord Heaven. He can't do anything about the insect pests either. What about his own kind? That depends. We don't want to live a shabby life. So we will have to be bandits. A bandit is someone who holds up travellers in the glare of daylight; a bandit is someone who is not afraid of death and dares to kill when the situation forces his hand. Lead your donkeys out and pick up any scrap that can serve as a weapon – something made of iron is best. Listen to what I'm saying: no pickaxes, hoes and scythes. These things are partly iron, but one glimpse tells people they are farm tools. Best if it's a hammer or a chopper. With these donkeys and those arms, we will be a gang."

"What should we do about our women and children?" someone asked.

"Leave them behind to watch over the village and the compounds," Wu answered. "When we have something to eat and drink, we'll be our own masters. They can then join us or we can come back to take up farming again."

Earthen Jar again rose to his feet. "Uncle, my wife has been at my home for barely a year."

"Yanking at your balls. If we're a gang, there can be none of this uncle business. We should have a chief. Listen to what I'm saying: I am old and I can't be the chief. Even so, we should have one. How? You fellas, look outside…"

Two wooden buckets stood outside the grass shelter. They were almost overflowing with cool water.

"Whoever can bear to down a bucketful of cold water will be our chief," the old man proposed.

The other eleven stared at the containers and Wu studied their reactions.

Earthen Jar swallowed a mouthful of spittle and shifted his eyes away from the buckets to look at Profound Meditation.

"Keen to try, are you?"

"I'm not," was Earthen Jar's reply.

"Don't look at me then."

"Don't goad me."

"Your tiny little stomach couldn't hold it anyhow."

"You are goading me."

Profound Meditation Wu brushed him aside.

"You are goading me again."

Profound Meditation Wu continued to brush him aside. Earthen Jar stood up.

"One bucket or two?" Earthen Jar demanded.

"One."

Earthen Jar ducked his head to size up his stomach and then walked over to Wu with another question: "If I were chosen as chief, could I bring my wife with me?"

"You can't."

Earthen Jar again took a look at his stomach and, after a moment of meditation, asked: "Do the chief's words count?"

"That depends. We still have a military adviser."

"Who is this military adviser?"

"Me."

Earthen Jar pondered for a while and said: "So be it. But I have another question: who is the biggest boss, the chief or the military adviser?"

"The chief."

"I really have been goaded. When the locusts are provoked, they gang up together and when I am provoked, I only want to gulp down that bucket of cool water."

"No matter how many words you spew out right now, it still amounts to nothing more than yanking at your balls. Striding over to those buckets is taking action."

Earthen Jar paced over to the pails. When he reached them, he again fired off a question without looking at Profound Meditation Wu: "When the chief and the military adviser lock horns, whose words should the gang members follow?"

"The chief's."

"You all heard this!" Earthen Jar shouted to the others in the grass shelter.

With heroic earnestness inscribed all over his face, Earthen Jar knelt down in front of the wooden buckets. He fixed his eyes on the cool water while massaging his stomach. He stared and massaged for a very long time. He knew it would not be easy to pour a whole bucketful into his stomach – it might even be impossible.

"You've stared and rubbed for too long," Profound Meditation Wu said. "No matter how much you stare, the cold water will never evaporate and no matter how much you rub, your stomach won't get any bigger."

Earthen Jar turned his head and seemed ready to weep. "You are goading me again," he growled at Wu.

"You are yanking at your balls again."

"OK, I'll stop yanking at my balls and drink." He started to guzzle.

Gu dong – he took one mouthful. *Gu dong* – he took another.

No one looked at Earthen Jar except for Profound Meditation Wu. They were all listening though.

Gu dong. Gu dong.

Not more than half of the bucketful of cool water had been downed.

Gu dong ... Gu dong ...

The intervals between each *gu dong* were growing longer and the sound weaker. Apparently Earthen Jar was now sucking in the water mouthful by mouthful.

"You can't polish off a whole bucketful by supping," Profound Meditation Wu insisted. "You should hold up the bucket and tip it down your throat."

Earthen Jar withdrew his head from inside the wooden bucket. He didn't look at Profound Meditation Wu but remained focused on the cool water. "What is it to you whether I sup or tip? Either way, it will all end up in my belly."

He buried his head in the wooden bucket once again.

It was already too painful for him to try to consume any more. The *gu dong* sound told the others just how excruciating it was. It seemed as if Earthen Jar was not drinking cool water but enduring torture. He could stand it no longer.

Gu ... dong.

He withdrew his mouth from the cool water but still buried his head in the wooden bucket. Apparently he wanted to take a break.

"I won't call you uncle anymore, but Profound Meditation Wu," he groaned. "The insect pests didn't screw me to death but you managed it with cold water."

Wu turned a deaf ear to his words and so did the rest of the crew. Their faces were cloudy – always cloudy.

Earthen Jar again crammed his mouth into the liquid.

Profound Meditation Wu creased his brow because he could sense a change in the sound of Earthen Jar's drinking. It was no longer the *gu dong* of before. He stood in front of Earthen Jar and cried out: "You son of a jackass. You're taking one mouthful of water and then spitting it out. You are not drinking at all. No wonder it's not glugging."

He then turned to the men in the grass shelter and said: "This son of a jackass is taking one mouthful of water and then – *buh* – spitting it out. It doesn't get anywhere near his stomach."

Earthen Jar withdrew his head quickly this time and gaped at Profound Meditation Wu. The water had drenched his face and found its way into his eyes. His voice was no longer the same: "I've already drunk up to my Adam's apple and can't swallow even one more mouthful. One more mouthful will make me throw up what's already gone down. If I don't throw it up, I will die. Don't you believe me?"

Earthen Jar boohooed. He knelt down, resting his hands on the rim of the wooden bucket.

"I was thinking, if I can drink this bucket of cool water, the first thing I will do is change my military adviser, but my stomach didn't throw itself into the task. Why wouldn't you let me bring my wife with me?"

Earthen Jar's tears plopped down into the wooden bucket like pearls from a broken string.

Ninth Kid reached Earthen Jar in only a few paces. His feet were big, stout and heavy and thus landed steadily and forcefully. He was a fast walker. On the final step, he didn't lower his foot. Instead, he raised it higher and higher and booted Earthen Jar's backside.

Earthen Jar had not expected an arse-kicking. With a *humph*, he wanted to turn his head and see who the attacker was. But his body lunged forward onto the wooden bucket, causing it – and him – to topple over. He lay belly-up, hiccuping, in the better part of a bucketful of water that he had failed to drink. Every time he hiccupped, he spurted out a mouthful of cool liquid. He no longer cried. He wasn't in the mood to find out who had kicked him either. He was spewing out water with his mouth agape.

Ninth Kid lifted the other wooden bucket.

The sound made by Ninth Kid when he poured the cool water into his throat was very clear.

The hemp stalk-like Profound Meditation Wu briefly blinked his small eyes rapidly and then told the spectators in the grass shelter: "Go bring your donkeys out."

They all rose to their feet. Nobody cared if Ninth Kid really could pour that whole bucketful of cool water into his stomach.

Not forgetting Earthen Jar, who was slumped in the muddy slush, Wu yelled: "You hear me?"

He was still regurgitating water and nodded while continuing to writhe.

3.

The donkey-back gang marched towards the Southeast. They believed there was copious rainfall in that region, which was beneficial for arable farming.

The comrades enforced one precept: no matter where they went and no matter who they encountered, they should wear a nasty expression. It was not so difficult because the locusts had already turned their faces sour. On the contrary, Profound Meditation Wu was being far-sighted: when they had something to eat and drink their guise of nastiness might slip. Therefore, this rule must be maintained.

Three months later, they upgraded their armoury – the hammers and choppers brought from home were exchanged for swords, each of which had a devil's head inscribed on the handle. The swords could protect their gallbladders. As every hero knew, the seat of their courage was this organ, not their balls. When necessary, the blades could also claim the lives of others.

Half a year later, they took in a hare hunter. He had his own homemade gun. In private they called him the "hare hunter" but in company they addressed him as the "self-taught marksman". Now they had not only iron wares but also a firearm too. They really had formed a detachment good and proper.

A donkey-back gang was a donkey-back gang. It was best if there were no other livestock mixed in with them. They therefore procured a mount for the hare hunter as well. It was no great undertaking for them to get a donkey. They just needed to flex their hands at an opportune moment.

Several days after the gang hit the road, Ninth Kid allocated a special task to Earthen Jar. He ordered him to memorise all the villages they marched past and all the taverns they boarded at, including their names and locations and the routes taken to reach them.

"Why?" Earthen Jar probed.

"No reason," Ninth Kid answered.

"You are just required to do it. Do whatever you are required to do. Less questions and more action."

"But we go past villages and go into taverns together. Everybody should do their share. Why thrust this chore on me?"

"Because you are the youngest and your mind is the most nimble."

"A nimble mind should keep the accounts book."

"That is down to Profound Meditation Wu. You just need to memorise the names of the villages and taverns for us."

"Fair enough. You are the chief. If you say something is a nail, it must be made of iron. Here at your beck and call."

"But you should never jumble them up."

"Never. But I must get one thing clear first: do you mean the villages we have passed by or the villages we have gone through?"

"Both."

"We pass by far more villages than we go through," gasped Earthen Jar. "But I'll be sure not to muddle them up in my mind. Didn't you say I have an agile mind? I agree."

Before going to bed every night, Earthen Jar would mentally revisit all the villages they passed and all the taverns at which they had boarded. It was never taxing. Not only was it not taxing, it actually proved very enjoyable – thrilling even – because when he was done going through the list, he could revivify some situations without any effort. He could savour again the enjoyment of the gang easily laying their hands on food, drink and money. It was quite a lark. It thrilled him to recall a time when they had turned ill luck into good and transformed peril into security.

However, this re-experiencing of enjoyment and thrills would turn out to be short-lived. They were marching past more and more villages and boarding at more and more taverns. Earthen Jar's brain could no longer bear it. On top of lodging in his mind the names of the villages and the taverns, he needed to pinpoint their locations and routes of access. There were so many village and tavern names plus the locations and routes. They were in danger of becoming stirred up in his mind like a wok of porridge. If that happened, he would not be able to answer to Ninth Kid.

"My brain is out of control," he told the chief. "I can't stand it anymore and my heart is out of whack as well. Every night in my mind I have to retrace my footsteps back to those villages and taverns like putting on a puppet show while you lot are fast asleep like pigs," he protested. "If this torment lasts much longer I'll get mental damage."

He told Ninth Kid to find another recruit. "It's not the harm to your body that scares me," he said. "I'm scared that I might screw up your business."

Ninth Kid asked Profound Meditation Wu for advice.

With a smile, Profound Meditation Wu chided Earthen Jar: "You son of a jackass, your stomach is lousy and so is your brain."

"Don't smile at me," said Earthen Jar. "You are bony and so is your face. No matter how you force out a smile, you don't look like a kind, honest man. If you must beat someone, don't strike out at his face; if you want to curse at someone, don't dish the dirt."

"If your brain is addled. Find something else to take its place."

"You really are silver-tongued. If it was your brain that was addled, could you think of something that would take its place?"

"Find a piece of brown paper to draw everything on."

Earthen Jar slapped his forehead and gasped: "Yeah, why did I never think of brown paper? Just having brown paper is not enough though. I need a writing brush and some ink so I can draw. This is still not good. Am I meant to bring a writing brush and an inkstone with me just for the sake of that one piece of brown paper? An inkstone is quite a lump."

"Every village has a scribe or scholar and you can get a writing brush and ink from them. You just need to keep a piece of brown paper about you and that's it."

Earthen Jar slapped his forehead once again and said: "I'm convinced; I am convinced. I will look for brown paper." He duly managed to lay his hands on a piece.

From then on, after they had eaten and drunk their fill in a certain tavern at a certain village, Earthen Jar would go here and there foraging for a writing brush and ink so as to scrawl marks on the brown paper and write down names of the villages and taverns. If there were any characters he didn't know how to write, he would pick Profound Meditation Wu's brain. He fashioned his jottings into a map.

As the donkey-back gang marched on, the brown paper became almost completely filled with scribbled pictures. Even so, Ninth Kid maintained that they ought to find a suitable place before setting down a foothold.

"If we can't find a base soon I'll need another piece of brown paper," Earthen Jar whinged.

"Make the pictures smaller and the paper will last a while longer," came the answer.

"How nice it would be if I didn't need to draw on it. I do despair at the things you say."

Earthen Jar had once asked Profound Meditation Wu provocatively: "You said before that as soon as we had something to eat and drink, we would bring our women or go home. Didn't you?"

"Yep. What's the matter?"

"I thought that you had clean forgotten about it."

"Never."

"Then I will ask you again. Can we say that we have something to eat and drink now?"

Wu didn't answer Earthen Jar's question. "Go bother Ninth Kid."

Earthen Jar didn't ask Ninth Kid this particular question. But in Profound Meditation Wu's absence, he did share something with their chief in private: "Profound Meditation Wu promised that we would either fetch our women or go back when we have something to eat and drink. The way I see it, he has never thought of doing this. The widow he was screwing for years has given him the heave ho and vanished without a trace. Who does he have to fetch now? He is a single man with only his prick. He is seeing a bit of the world while he helps us to stage our hold-ups. What does he have to scurry back home for? To farm the land? There is food and drink here. Why should he go home to farm? His situation is different from ours and so is his state of mind. I have a woman and you even have children. We've been holding-up and robbing people for so long. Don't we have some savings by now? You only let us seize people's wealth but never their women. You order us to hold back and tough it out. Isn't this because you still hope we can take a look at our women? I can't believe that you don't miss your woman at night. Profound Meditation Wu is pushing sixty, yet he still blurts out that he feels lustful after being stoked up and wrapped up warm. He is old and he can make do with it by simply saying so. We are hot-blooded and vigorous. Can we make ourselves stop missing women simply by saying so? I will be honest with you: I miss being with a woman every night."

Ninth Kid delivered his answer to Earthen Jar. "You son of a jackass, if you dare think about this and lay a finger on a woman anywhere, I will order the marksman to fire gunpowder and iron shot straight into your bastard face. Then you can go to King Yama's palace and deflower a ghost."

"Riches are just worldly possessions, but women are not," Ninth Kid explained. "We hold-up people everywhere we go, yet none of us has lost his life and not one person has been wounded. That's because we demand riches, but never women. You think that I don't want to? I wouldn't be a man if I didn't. But do I dare? That thing of yours isn't made out of iron. It won't ever get rusty, no matter how long it goes unused. We haven't reached the right place or saved enough. We must continue on the road. You should stick to marking your brown paper."

"I got it. My mouth is fond of spouting words that are like gas – thin and flavourless. Don't get angry with me. Hurry up and look: that marksman is taking aim and getting ready to fire."

The donkey-back gang halted. From their mounts, they studied the marksman. His posture when aiming was very special. It was not his habit to clutch the homemade gun with one hand at the front and the other at the rear, then aim forward. Instead, he reached out both arms straight and held his gun horizontally with the mouth of the barrel aimed to one side. By rights, this should not be called as "aiming at" but "targeting". He relied on intuition rather than eyesight. When he felt that the quarry was in the target, he found his precise aim. Then the index finger of his right hand hooked backwards and – *bang* – he never missed.

Ninth Kid delighted in watching how the marksman focused and shot like this. Holding a jerry-made firearm in this manner was no skill in itself. The knack lay in gripping the weapon in just such a way and then hitting the victim without fail. The marksman had such a marvellous skill. He explained that this knack was forced upon him by the hares. Hares won't crouch down in front of you as sitting ducks do. What should you do if you catch it out of the corner of your eye? You could turn around but it would scarper before you had chance to take aim. It would run willy-nilly, giving you no time to find your target, then disappear and leave you dizzy. How would you feel holding a homemade gun in your hands with your head spinning? The hare had played you like a monkey. "For that reason," the self-taught marksman concluded, "I never turn blindly. I never pivot my body; I only adjust my gun."

Now the donkey-mounted shooter was again holding his homemade gun horizontally with both arms reaching out straight.

Their eyes followed the barrel of the rifle to its likely target. Not far away there was an earthen platform rank with weeds and, seemingly, a Mongolian gazelle hiding among the foliage. They pulled the reins of their donkeys taut to prevent them from raising their hooves, lest the deer might be startled.

Bang.

The Mongolian gazelle was gone.

Earthen Jar slapped the rear of his mount so he could be the first one to gallop over to the prey. The area was not in fact covered with weeds. Only its perimeter was overgrown with grass. The platform acted as a winnowing ground. The wheat stalks piled at its centre had already been crushed numerous times by the grinding stone, leaving a residue of chaff. The muzzled donkey whose job it had been to turn the stone stood on the wheat straw, appearing very quiet and solitary. The beast had been relieved of the burden of rotating that mill for all eternity. Its driver was gone.

Slain by the homemade gun, its master's body had tumbled down into the clump of weeds at the edge of the earthen platform. The donkey was not perturbed in the least by the discharging firearm.

The gang all clambered onto the patch and crowded around the victim.

"That's no Mongolian gazelle," Earthen Jar told Ninth Kid.

Ninth Kid didn't utter a sound and his bristling side-whiskers were all dust and dirt.

None of them spoke, their faces grimy as they rode on.

Their mounts were animals when all was said and done, incapable of tuning into human affairs. A number of them not only flared their nostrils but also swayed on their hooves at leisure. The donkey at the centre of the winnowing ground was stirred to scratch with its fore-hooves so as to indicate that it stood among their kind.

Earthen Jar jumped down and straightened out the curled-up body of the deceased. The old man's trousers were hitched down as low as his knees, leaving his backside exposed. Earthen Jaw then spotted a puddle of faeces and urine.

He caught on and told the marksman: "This guy was taking a shit with his bum raised up high and you mistook him for a gazelle."

"His arse has been well and truly mauled. Now it looks like a hornet's nest," he added.

"Holy shit, why is his face messed up as well? Oh, oh, I got it, I got it now. When you aimed at him, he was gawping back at you from below his upturned arse. He bared his bum and his face at you together."

He then gave his summing up. "If he hadn't been peeping at you he might not have been killed. His butt could still have been blasted up to blazes, but it wouldn't have cost him his life. Hitting the head and face was what was lethal. He mustn't have been expecting a shot from a homemade gun. If he had, he surely wouldn't have contorted like that."

The marksman was in an awkward position. "My eyes were playing tricks on me," he implored Ninth Kid.

Ninth Kid apparently did not hear. Instead, he was scanning around. Since the wheat stalks had been threshed and the grain taken home, heaps of chaff were everywhere.

"He must be from the village at the bottom of the slope," reasoned the marksman. "What should we do?"

Ninth Kid and Profound Meditation Wu confided in each other and came to a conclusion.

"This was his fate," Ninth Kid proposed.

"I agree," Wu said.

"A good harvest."

"Look at those stacks of straw."

"This place produces decent grain."

"All wheat, as it happens."

Ninth Kid and Wu compared notes for a while and then struck upon an idea.

"Untether the donkey," Ninth Kid ordered Earthen Jar.

"Put the dead man on the donkey," he then instructed

the comrades. "It knows the way and will head back to the village with its rider."

"What should we do?"

"We'll smoke a pipeful of tobacco and then enter the village once the donkey reaches home," was Ninth Kid's reply.

He emphasised especially that the dead man's arse should be tilted skywards so that the onlookers would first spot the hornet nest-like posterior riddled with iron shot.

The others immediately felt tense.

The shooter was no exception. Ninth Kid slapped his shoulder and consoled him by insisting: "Take it easy. Load your gun with powder and shot. I'll be watching you." He crouched down in front of him.

"You should alter your hare-hunting position and aim straight forward."

A round of drum, gong and *suona* horn music emanated from the village at the bottom of the slope.

Earthen Jar slapped the donkey, now weighed down with the corpse. It raised its hooves and clambered down from the earthen platform.

Ninth Kid and his men also mounted their donkeys and assumed the scowl they had been drilled into wearing.

4.

The villagers were celebrating a bumper harvest.

The village was nestled at the bottom of the slope and consisted of nearly a hundred households. It was a hamlet that reclined against the mountains and overlooked a river. The river that zigzagged out of the highlands and girdled the community appeared to have swept clear a patch of earth especially for the residents to occupy. Having accomplished that singular feat, it babbled onwards undeterred. Wherever the channel snaked its course, level fertile farmland was created. "Go up to the mountains, cut firewood, go across the river and strip yourself nude." When this saying was spoken in another place, it became tinged with a measure of futility, the gist being that mere mortals had to follow the orders of the heavens and bow to their fate. But if this saying was repeated locally, it took on a gloating quality. It epitomised the geographical advantages of the village and the easy and carefree life to be had there. In different places, the same words conveyed starkly contrasting meanings.

The village was called Ancestral Worshippers Shrine. That name affirmed that the natives knew they should be thankful; they should express gratitude to their ancestors for having chosen such a fine place and give thanks to the heavens, the earth and the gods for allowing their forbears to settle down here permanently and multiply in number. At Chinese New Year and every other festival, the locals would burn incense sticks and offer sacrifices to thank their ancestors. Every time the grain had been brought back into their granaries, they would organise people to ply gongs, beat drums, blow *suona* horns, walk on stilts and jockey about bamboo hobbyhorses. Their instruments and limbs became novelties to please the heavens, the earth and the gods, and to amuse themselves by the by.

The conductor of the gong, drum and *suona* horn band was Heavenly Music Zhao, the Village Head. He brandished a pair of drumsticks wrapped in red satin, drawing beautiful arcs in the air like two flowers. The leading stilt-walker was his son, Steamed Bun. In their elaborate costumes, with their faces painted brilliantly and with long, thin willow wood stilts bound to their legs, they followed the gongs, drums and *suona* horns to trace circuits around the village streets. A skilful stilt-walker would walk elegantly, as if he were dancing in all kinds of gaits, while constantly winking flirtatiously at the women, to the amusement of onlookers. The sight of someone falling flat on his face would immediately elicit merry shouts and raucous laughter.

Almost all the villagers were on the street. They had forgotten about Old Fourth Ren working outside the village. Much less would they have expected that as they were shouting and laughing, he would be carried back to them draped across the back of a clattering donkey. This promptly brought their gongs, drums and *suona* horns to a standstill as well as gagging their mouths.

The first to catch sight of the donkey and the slain man was Neighing Horse, apprentice to the cobbler Righteous Kindness Zhou. Neighing Horse was only fifteen and had a speech impediment. While watching the clamour, he felt fit to burst and sought out a spot where he could empty his bladder without having to remove his gaze from the festivities. He ambled to the entrance to the village. The community had no gates and was exposed to the world. The entrance presented a suitable spot to take his monster leak with his back to the village, while all the time keeping his head cocked so as to scan the village street.

In hindsight, stuttering Neighing Horse really was a poor wretch. His plan had been canny but unfortunately foundered. Barely had he unfastened his cloth belt when he saw Old Fourth Ren's donkey. Next he spotted the owner slung over its back. Then came the arse cheeks that had been mutilated by the homemade gun. Moments later, the bandit gang drew into view.

Not one drop of urine was released. It stayed tightly clamped in his ducts. Neighing Horse hitched up his trousers and cloth belt, scooted back into the village with his eyebrows askew and his eyes bulging and intercepted the marching army of stilt-walkers who were waddling about with all kinds of gaits. Terrified and panic-stricken, he spared no efforts in making his mouth twitch but failed to splutter even one word. His hands didn't know how they should gesticulate either. From high up on his stilts, Steamed Bun grew agitated.

"Sing it out!" he shouted at the lad.

Neighing Horse immediately broke into a ditty which went, "*Yi a ai*, the bandits – the bandits have sho, sho, *a ma*, shot Ren, *ai*, to death!"

The villagers' dissolute laughter died a death and then so too did the drum music. All of the people stood rooted in the street, turning their heads to the entrance of the village.

Ninth Kid's mob had already lined up at the gate; their thirteen donkeys forming a very neat configuration with all hooves remaining fastened to the ground.

The only creature to stir belonged to Old Fourth Ren. *Clatter, clatter*, it trotted forward at leisure, neither fast nor slow.

Finally, the beast of burden halted.

The villagers could now clearly make out Old Fourth Ren as well as Old Fourth Ren's arse. The order in which they perceived things echoed Neighing Horse's example.

Nobody shrieked. Their facial expressions revealed that they were initially puzzled and then terrified. Their gaze shifted from Old Fourth Ren's backside to the faces of the bandits. The outlaws wore coarse dirty countenances like pieces of raw iron.

In timely fashion, the marksman reached for his already-loaded rifle. He didn't hold it horizontally, instead aiming straight ahead.

Neighing Horse clutched the waist of his trousers and his cloth belt in his hands. He hadn't done it up yet. Not being able to hold on any longer, a yellow flow spilled soundlessly from his crotch, forming a pool on the ground.

No one delved into the reason why the bandits had killed Old Fourth Ren. It was not because they didn't want to. They had no opportunity – they were all gripped by mortal dread. They and the vagabonds stared at each other on the village street at length. Suddenly someone let out a *wah!* The villagers then scrambled into a melee. They discarded their gongs and drums and other musical instruments, not to mention the willow wood stilts, and then took to their heels. Within the blink of an eye, only Heavenly Music Zhao was left on the street with Old Fourth Ren's donkey. As Village Head, he stood alone as everyone else dispersed. No longer staring at the interlopers, he tossed aside his drumsticks and walked up to the donkey, giving it a single gentle slap. The animal then made a beeline to Old Fourth Ren's home, for it knew not only the route but also the correct door.

Old Fourth Ren's family didn't want to ruffle feathers by hunting down the slayer. As carefully and painstakingly as possible, they plucked out some of the iron shot that had become lodged in his face with a pair of tweezers – not every last fragment because much of it had punctured into the subcutaneous depths and if it were all extracted the results would be unsightly. There was no need to prod out the shot from his arse. After he was dressed, it could no longer be seen and his image would not be influenced. Old Fourth Ren was clad in his shroud and placed in a coffin. He was already pushing seventy. His sons and daughters had prepared his winding sheet and casket long before. These were customs handed down from their forebears at Ancestral Worshippers Shrine. When a man reached an advanced age, his burial accoutrements should be assembled beforehand and put on standby.

Similarly, Heavenly Music Zhao the Village Head didn't want to call the bandits to account. But he implemented a series of decisions. First of all, he arranged for Ninth Kid and his band to settle down in the village office. Secondly, he called on some fellow villagers who had holed themselves up and told them to prepare wine and a meal for the donkey-back band. Thirdly, he went to Old Fourth Ren's home to offer up both verbal and material condolences. Ren's unforeseen passing would be handled as though he had died during a business trip. The expenditure for his burial ceremony would be shared out evenly among his fellow villagers.

"Why did they shoot him dead?" the family wanted to know.

"You should ask them," he replied. Then added: "I can enquire on your behalf, but I am afraid that it would give rise to more serious trouble. So, my advice is that we should keep it buttoned."

"Fair's fair then, we won't."

"Take care of his final affairs. I still need to go to the village office. The rice and dishes are almost ready. I should call them over to drink and dine."

Two tables were set. According to the ancestral customs and table etiquette, a dinner table for entertaining guests should seat six diners plus one local villager, whose duty it was to greet the guests, take care of them and accompany them in their drinking. This villager should take the seat opposite the seats of honour. The gang had thirteen members. Two tables would entertain twelve of them and one more was left behind. Heavenly Music Zhao instructed that a third table should be laid according to the practice. "There is no need," Earthen Jar said. "I will take the seat opposite the seats of honour to replace the guy who should have come to keep us company. You shouldn't take this as flouting custom." Ninth Kid, moreover, insisted there was no need to lay a third table and that two were enough.

Heavenly Music Zhao no longer stood his ground, saying: "Then that brother must have received the short end of the stick."

"Not at all, not at all," answered Earthen Jar. "Let's dig in."

It was a square meal with decent liquor to boot. They were already ravenous and tempted to hack away like wolves. But before the meal, Profound Meditation Wu had impressed on them that they should dine as politely as possible. Consequently, they savoured the food with impeccable manners. While wining and dining, Ninth Kid chatted with Heavenly Music Zhao. One portion of their dialogue went as follows:-

"Are you the Village Head?"

"Indeed."

"Your place is nice."

"Yeah."

"Your ancestors had sharp eyes."

"For sure."

"You should always keep in mind the favour that they did for you."

"Yeah. That's the reason why it's called Ancestral Worshippers Shrine."

"Why a 'shrine' and not a 'village'?"

"The heavens, the earth and the gods are lodged in our minds too."

"Oh, oh. Many scholars must have come out of here?"

"We set great store by both tilling and studying. We are households of farmers and scholars."

"Are there any renowned men of letters now?"

"It is said that there once were. That must have been a long time ago."

"Can you be counted as a man of letters?"

"No. Each generation is weaker than the one before. My grandpa gave me the name *Heavenly Music*. My father gave his grandson the name *Steamed Bun*. We are retreating further away from the world of letters and making our mouths the boss."

"A steamed bun is filling. We wandered here only for the sake of our mouths."

"Everyone is just the same. You might live your life this way and that. But, at the end of the day, you live for your mouth. You come from faraway and you still need to go a very great distance. Eat and drink to your hearts' content. Thanks to the Old Lord Heaven, this place is blessed with mild winds and plenty of rain. The weather this year has been especially fair. We have brought home more grain.

Even if we hadn't, we would still do our best to entertain our guests who have come from afar. This is the custom bequeathed by our ancestors."

"Oh, oh."

5.

Ninth Kid refused Heavenly Music Zhao the Village Head's hospitality and didn't stay in the village office overnight. Rather, he took shelter in the Heaven and Earth Temple outside the settlement together with his donkey-back gang. Ninth Kid told Heavenly Music Zhao to put his heart at ease. He swore that the animals in his gang were all well-trained. After they had eaten and drunk their fill, they would be very quiet and would refrain from shitting or pissing carelessly. The temple wouldn't be soiled. They would just bed down in the halls without laying a finger on anything sacred. In that way, the deities in the halls would be left undisturbed.

In fact, not all of them chose the halls of the temple. Only Ninth Kid and Profound Meditation Wu settled in the main hall. The marksman and Earthen Jar took it in turns to catch some shuteye at a spot three feet away from the rear gate of the temple. The baker's dozen of donkeys were tethered behind the main hall and attended by two henchmen; in the event of anything happening, they would unleash the steeds immediately. The remaining seven men were in the front courtyard and could sleep anywhere. After making clear his arrangements, Ninth Kid again commanded them: "No matter where you lie, make sure your stuff is within ready reach."

By *stuff*, Ninth Kid meant their swords.

Normally, they would have slept tight here for the night, but Ninth Kid couldn't drop off despite turning this way and that a dozen or more times. "What's going on? Still restless. Really!" he complained. Profound Meditation Wu, who was sleeping at the other end, didn't react. Ninth Kid no longer turned this way and that but sat up and mumbled: "Why is the moon so bright?" Profound Meditation Wu murmured not a sound. Ninth Kid got up and left the main hall.

After a while, he came back with Earthen Jar on his tail.

"It is midnight already," Earthen Jar moaned. "You didn't wake me up early and you didn't wake me up late. You chose the exact moment I was half-asleep in a trance. The two of us should take turns to kip, my elder brother. You can't fall asleep but I can."

Ninth Kid told Earthen Jar to light the two big candles on the offertory table. "I heard you tell the Village Head that we wouldn't lay a finger on anything in the temple," the younger man said.

"The candles are normally lit to worship their gods, but we're borrowing a touch of that light since it is there."

"You ought to find it harder to fall asleep with that light dazzling your eyes."

"You son of a jackass."

"Oh, oh, I shall do it, I shall do it."

Earthen Jar lit the wicks.

"I want light not because I want to sleep but because I want to look at the brown paper," Ninth Kid explained. "Take it out for me."

"There is no need to look at it. After the dinner party was over, I lost no time in finding a writing brush and ink and scrawled down *Ancestral Worshippers Shrine*."

"You churn out more words than you do shit. Get a move on," rebuked Ninth Kid. Earthen Jar brought out the piece of brown paper.

"Bring the candle closer," Ninth Kid ordered. Earthen Jar took one candle from its candlestick to illuminate the paper for him.

Ninth Kid stared at it long and hard.

"If you want to look at it, look at it carefully and don't let your mind wander," Earthen Jar reminded.

Ninth Kid was really a little absent-minded. "OK," he said. "I give up. Stash away the paper, put the candle back where it belongs and go back to where you were crashing."

Earthen Jar went away. Profound Meditation Wu sat up.

"I've woken you up," Ninth Kid said.

"I never fell asleep."

"Oh, oh."

"I was listening and trying to read your mind."

"Oh, oh."

"You've got something on your mind."

"That's right."

"When you chatted with the Village Head at the wine table, I could tell. When you ordered over Earthen Jar to study the brown paper, my suspicion was confirmed. Your heart is on edge."

"Yeah."

"You can't force yourself to sleep. What say we go and hang around outside?"

They went outside the temple, sitting for a spell staring at the not-so-distant mountains, at Ancestral Worshippers Shrine at the bottom of the slope, and at the waters of the babbling river that snaked out of the mountains. The Heaven and Earth Temple stood on the elevated plateau at the bend of the river. The moon was clear and bright. The moonlit river was similarly clear and bright.

Then they started to talk.

"It is a nice place no matter how you look at it," surmised Ninth Kid.

Profound Meditation Wu agreed.

"They share the same moon with us?"

"The same one."

"And the same sun?"

"The same one. There is only one moon and one sun in the sky. And we haven't gone beyond the sky."

"Since we are all under the same sun and moon, how come they have been given such a fine spot?"

"They are blessed."

"We can't go beyond the sky?"

"Impossible. There are skies beyond the sky."

"Then should we keep on moving? We can't keep rolling forever."

"That depends. But it is risky for bandits to sit tight somewhere."

"If we could sit tight somewhere, we would no longer be bandits. Bandits who flee hither and thither are bandits forever."

"You have made up your mind?"

"I want to hear your opinion. If I had made up my mind, I would have gone to sleep."

"This is not our home village."

"Of all the food, drink and lodgings we have had along the way, what actually belonged to us? No matter, we've still eaten, drunk and laid our heads."

"Just in case."

"Just in case, just in case, just in case!"

"Don't be agitated. Being constantly on the road is different from sitting tight and being somewhere. We can still eat, drink, bed down and take away those things that don't belong to us because we are always on our way. It would not be that simple if we wanted to sit tight somewhere. We should find a seat first. But what if we can't?"

"We can take to the road again."

"What if we can't do either?"

"I can't understand what you're driving at."

"Then listen carefully. If we sit tight here, we have them in our clutches. When we have them in our clutches, we have succeeded in sitting tight, which means nothing serious will happen. If we can't sit tight here, we haven't got them in our clutches. If we can't have them in our clutches, nothing will be certain for us. Think over my words. We have only thirteen guys but there are more than two hundred people in this village. I have made it very straight and clear. If I still need to say more, my words will turn unpleasant. Just think about the locusts. They just whooshed over without informing us and without any omens. Can you react in time?"

Ninth Kid pondered over the locusts at length.

"I was still mumbling in my mind before you mentioned the locusts," said Ninth Kid. "But bringing them up really shook me awake. One trample of your foot is enough to make a pest pie. You can trample and trample again. But no matter how many locusts you trample to death, the rest of the swarm won't be deterred. *You go on with your trampling and I'll continue my gnawing. If your foot lands on me, I'm a goner; if your foot doesn't land on me, I'll go on gnawing forever.* They are locusts. They don't know what life is, they don't know what death is and they don't know what fear is. But men are different. They know what life is, they know what death is and they know what fear is. We can at least cherish life somehow."

Profound Meditation Wu started to blink. "Carry on. Your words are starting to show a bit of spice. Continue."

"We shouldn't only think about what happens if we can't sit tight here. We should also think about what if we can sit tight here."

"The more you talk, the more I feel that we can sit tight here. Continue."

"If they are scared of death and afraid to lose their lives, no matter how great their number is, they are still alone, not a pile, not a gang. One homemade gun can make them obey us."

"Continue, continue."

"Should anyone throw himself into our line of fire or lunge at our swords, we forfeit our lives."

"OK, stop there." Profound Meditation Wu stood up. "You have reasoned it out and got to the bottom of it. Do you need to continue?"

"No, I am through."

Ninth Kid rose to his feet as well: "If I still need to say something more, I shall have words with them."

6.

That same night, Heavenly Music Zhao the Village Head had a talk with his son as well.

He was reluctant to speak to anyone, Steamed Bun included. After inviting the bandits to the banquet, then escorting them to the Heaven and Earth Temple, he no longer had the desire to converse. On his way back home, many fellow villagers addressed him as Village Head at their respective gates along the street. They called out very cautiously. He knew they wanted to enquire about something and keep abreast of the situation. His only response was an "En," an "Ah" or an "Oh". He didn't pause; he simply entered his compound directly. There were at least two reasons for this disengagement. The first was that none of them called him Village Head when the bandits entered the village. Why did they all disappear, squeaking like mice that have caught sight of a cat, and leaving him – the Village Head – alone on the street? After they knew he had smoothed things over with the bandits, why did they scuttle out from behind their gates like rapacious rodents and start calling him Village Head? The vermin should have a fellow mouse as Village Head, not Heavenly Music Zhao. Secondly, from the moment he tossed aside his drumsticks and slapped the donkey carrying Old Fourth Ren's body, didn't they know how the Village Head managed to tough it out? Did they think that they had a monopoly on feeling mortal dread? To paraphrase this crudely: his prick and balls had been scared upstairs. Every inch of his body – from his head to his toes and from the inside to the outside, including even his scalp – was being pulled taut. And how long would that last? Is there anything more laborious and nerve-racking in this world than having to cope with bandits?

He gave the cold shoulder not only to his fellow villagers, but to his family too, including his father Modest Zhao and his wife. When he stepped over the threshold, they crowded round him. He raised a palm towards them. Mouths that had been opened wide in curiosity were promptly gagged and they choked back the questions that were already on the tips of their tongues. He acted the same way towards his son Steamed Bun, collapsing on the brick bed, shutting his eyes and going to sleep.

"Leave it," Steamed Bun's mother whispered. "He's come back safe and sound so there's no need to keep on badgering. He wants to sleep, so let him sleep. We should all turn in ourselves."

Steamed Bun didn't obey her words. "It's barely nightfall and too early for bed," he scoffed. "How can I fall asleep?" Perching on the edge of his parents' *kang*, he insisted that he would wait until his father woke up.

"Your father is spent and broken. He might sleep tight until daybreak."

"No, he won't. He can't rest in this state." He cast a glance at his father's face and continued: "Even though father's eyes are closed, his lids keep twitching. That goes to prove that what I've said is true."

"Grandpa and grandma can't get any shuteye either," he added. "Few folks in this village can. Mother, what about you?"

Heavenly Music Zhao sat up with a start. "Listen up: whether I am able to sleep tight or not, you should at least give me the chance to try and drop off. I certainly can't manage it with you bearing down on me, croaking like a toad."

Heavenly Music Zhao went to the privy, laying down again when he returned.

Steamed Bun was very stubborn and sat tight on the edge of the *kang*, refusing to leave.

"The kid wants to talk," Zhao's wife said. "So you should say a few more words. If you don't, the boy won't go to bed. If he doesn't go to bed, I can't sleep tight either."

Heavenly Music Zhao shut his eyes. "There is nothing to talk about."

"There is." Steamed Bun was adamant.

His father sat up again. "With one squeak, a street full of people all vamoosed. They left me out there alone. You're my son, but you vanished too. I'm right, aren't I?"

"I thought you'd run away with them."

"If we all ran away, how could we deal with the bandits?"

"I went over to greet them during the banquet too. You didn't order me over there and I went off my own bat. That wasn't because you're the Village Head but because you are my father."

Steamed Bun's mother chipped in: "Yeah, yeah, the kid went there as well with his heart in his mouth."

Heavenly Music drew in a long draught until the air reached his navel and then exhaled slowly. Now, he no longer seemed reticent about talking.

"They spoiled a ripping round of gong and drum music to celebrate a good harvest," Steamed Bun whinged.

"Yet another stupid comment. Old Fourth Ren was already sprawled out on the back of that donkey. His family is trying to think up a way of burying him on the quiet, but you bring up gong and drum music."

"Fair enough, skip the gong and drum music. Let's talk about that mob. They've murdered a man and are acting as if they've done nothing."

"You can't think like this. You must follow the logic our ancestors observed: in the sky there are unexpected winds and clouds; in life there are unpredictable twists of fate."

"A debtor pays back his debt with money and a murderer pays for the life he took with his own – our ancestors observed that as well."

"Ah, ah, ah, ah!" Heavenly Music Zhao glared fixedly at Steamed Bun with his eyes wide open and his neck stiff. "How could your mind run awry like this? What are you using instead of brains?" he reproached. "Don't you know how risky that kind of thinking is?" He called out Steamed Bun's name and continued: "Don't you know, even though you are already nineteen and getting ready to be a husband, you're still an unripe melon." He didn't want anything unfortunate to happen, least of all to Steamed Bun. He called out his name again and lectured him: "The past three generations of our family have each only produced one son and heir. Your grandpa, grandma, father and mother are all hoping that you will marry a woman, sire your own young and bring new life into this world as soon as possible so this household can thrive. Hey!"

Heavenly Music Zhao now foamed at the mouth. The more he lectured, the more he felt that this event was significant. He thought that the froth alone was not sufficient to make the matter clear to his son. He believed that he should calm down and backtrack to discuss the topic again. He gave his mouth a wipe and composed himself.

"That proverb you put so eloquently – a debtor pays back his debt with money and a murderer pays for the life he took with his own – was sure enough left to us by our ancestors. However, did you consider that our ancestors spoke these words to men and not bandits?"

"Bandits are men too."

"Wrong!" his father snapped. "Bandits are men in one sense, but in another they are not."

He didn't allow Steamed Bun the opportunity to argue again. He needed him to listen.

"Men walk on human roads and bandits strut along the outlaw path. When bandits swagger on human roads, they are still men; when they strut along the outlaw path, they are bandits. They admitted that it was involuntary manslaughter, that they mistook Old Fourth Ren for a gazelle. Are they being truthful? We no longer have any way of looking into it. Why? The man is already dead so that part is done and dusted. What matters is that when they spoke, they were still talking in the language of human beings and walking on human roads. If you persist in investigating and apportioning blame, they won't speak the language of human beings anymore. Instead, they'll revert to the outlaw path. If they revert to the outlaw path, Old Fourth Ren's family won't be the only ones in this village who'll need to bury their own. You got it?

"Next I shall explain to you the bit about the second part of the proverb," he added. "Can we pay back a lost human life? Money and wealth can never compensate for a life unlawfully taken because human life cannot be measured by money, and money cannot be measured by human life. No matter how much money has been coughed up, can a dead man use it? If he could, he wouldn't be a dead man and there would be no need for compensation. Right or wrong? If you have the power, you can give the dead man another life – resuscitate Old Fourth Ren. But is that possible? A life claimed by a murderer can never be given back. I have seen *a life for a life* – using one life to atone for another. But do you want the bandits to pay for Old Fourth Ren's loss with one of theirs? Listen, you upstart, this is not the human way of thinking. Does anyone want to become another Old Fourth Ren? Do you? Do I? Don't hum and haw. Listen to me."

"I have done everything humanly possible," he continued. "I have been to Ren's home. I have laid two dinner tables for the bandits. I have arranged for them to rest their legs at the Heaven and Earth Temple. I haven't pushed them to revert to the outlaw path. Are there any better methods? After a hearty meal washed down with plenty of spirits and some decent shuteye, they'll hit the road again and go wherever they please. If you really want to keep your mind occupied, think about the business between you and Sprout."

Sprout was Steamed Bun's fiancée and Righteous Kindness Zhou the cobbler's daughter. She had yet to move into Steamed Bun's household as his bride.

7.

Sprout and her father Righteous Kindness Zhou were not afraid of the bandits because they had never actually clapped eyes on them. When the bandits entered the village, they had already gone back to their home along the street.

Righteous Kindness disliked big festive gatherings. "It's too messy, too messy," he complained. "The gongs and drums rattle my head till it aches. Let's go back, go back, go back."

"Let's watch for a bit longer," Sprout insisted.

Knowing that Sprout just really wanted to see Steamed Bun, Righteous Kindness Zhou remarked: "If you want to see someone on stilts, marry the lad and tell him to put on a private performance."

Sprout was still unwilling to head back. "You have only finished making one of the pair of embroidered sachets so there is another one to be made," her father pointed out. When the pouches were mentioned, Sprout followed him obediently.

A solitary reed mattress was spread out in the courtyard. Sprout sat cross-legged on it using silken threads to embroider flowers and birds onto the sachet. Her father was on the stone steps beneath the eaves clamping a pair of top plates between his legs and stitching the sole to the upper of a shoe.

"Father, ah, listen," Sprout piped up. "The gong and drum music has died down."

"Hark at you, you have been back here for an age and your mind is still on the street."

"Really it has. Listen." When Zhou was on the point of saying he was not bothered, the gate was slammed open by

Neighing Horse.

The boy, whose face was wax yellow, twisted his mouth and gesticulated with his hands. "The ban, ban ban ban …"

"Sing it out," his master prompted.

"*Yi a ai*, the bandits – shot Ren to, *a, ma*, to death!"

"Ah, ah, ah, really?"

"Really. Old Ren was, *a, me*, on the back of his donkey covered with blood …"

"Sing again."

"*Yi a ai*, gongs and drums had been, *a, me*, thrown all over the ground and people, *a, me*, had all run away."

Righteous Kindness Zhou and Sprout both became rather tense.

"What about Brother Steamed Bun?" Sprout demanded. Neighing Horse shook his head for all he was worth.

Righteous Kindness Zhou stood up to shut the gate and slid a carrying pole horizontally behind it.

His daughter cast down the sachet and thread and gripped Neighing Horse's shoulders. "Don't tremble. I am asking you how my Brother Steamed Bun is."

Neighing Horse's legs froze firm and his body shrank. "*Yi a ai*, I had no time, *ma*, to observe, *ai*. I had wetted, *me*, my crutch, wetted, *me*, my crutch. Pity, pity."

Now Sprout spotted Neighing Horse's damp patch and giggled. His wax-yellow face flushed cherry red. His body shrank further and seemed ready to recede into nothing. Sprout giggled more loudly and thudded down on the reed mattress.

"Tee-hee-hee," Righteous Kindness Zhou snarled.

"I won't laugh, I won't laugh," Sprout, still chuckling, said. "Hurry up and put on fresh trousers."

Neighing Horse went to get changed.

"You see, you see," her father surmised. "It's lucky we came back."

Sprout no longer laughed. "I am still fretting about Brother Steamed Bun," she wailed. "I will go to the street to have a look. I am not afraid." With these words, she prepared to draw back the carrying pole from the gate. Righteous Kindness Zhou let out a "hey" and blocked her way.

"You can't go out, no matter who you are worried about."

He told Sprout to wash Neighing Horse's trousers. While doing the laundry, Sprout muttered that she was anxious about her Brother Steamed Bun.

"You can worry about him now. But just stay at home and keep an ear to the stirrings outside."

They remained where they were, attentively auditing what was happening beyond their walls. In the process, they lent an ear to Neighing Horse, who brought them up to speed about the bandits and the donkey-back gang, about the homemade gun and the long blades, and about how Old Fourth Ren was slumped on the back of the donkey, his face and arse caked with blood. Sprout became even more knotted up about Steamed Bun.

"Stop, Neighing Horse," his master ordered. "Stop talking." He didn't want Sprout to worry. He commented on how his young apprentice had never seen one little bit of the world and thus everything new was jaw-dropping to him. The lad had merely overreacted.

After nightfall, the village finally stirred. Righteous Kindness Zhou wanted to dispatch his assistant to the street to scout around. Neighing Horse declined. Sprout volunteered, to which her father declared: "You can't go outside." He pulled back the carrying pole from the gate and went out himself.

They then learned that the Village Head had laid on a

banquet for the bandits and arranged for them to bed down at the Heaven and Earth Temple. They learned, moreover, that the Village Head had gone back home to sleep and so on and so forth. Sprout asked her father if he had seen her Brother Steamed Bun.

"Brother Steamed Bun, Brother Steamed Bun. You only have him in your heart! You worry about him, but he is now holed up at home with the doors bolted very, very tight. You're not frightened but they're scared out of their wits, don't you know?"

Righteous Kindness Zhou again slid the carrying pole home.

"I shan't worry about anybody and I shan't ever go out," Sprout retorted, and went back to her bedroom.

"Will the bandits kill more folks?" Neighing Horse asked his master.

"You should ask the bandits that."

"Oh, oh."

The two men shared the same kang.

After burrowing under the coverlet, Neighing Horse began again: "What should we do if the bandits want to kill people?"

"Even if they want to kill people, your turn will never come around. So, just nod off with an easy heart."

"Will your turn come soon?"

Righteous Kindness Zhou gave Neighing Horse a kick and snarled: "When the sky caves in, those ruffians will be able to prop them up. I am just a small fish."

"The sky will never cave in. You can be sure the bandits will kill people."

Righteous Kindness Zhou kicked Neighing Horse again and growled: "The Village Head will stand at the front shielding me, so how can I be killed?"

"Old Fourth Ren was not the Village Head."

"*Ai, ai*, what's wrong with you? Why do you keep on lumping the bandits and me together? I really want to belt you off this *kang*."

"I can't fall asleep. The bandits are always flashing in front of my eyes and I have butterflies in my stomach."

"Shut your eyes tight."

"I did but they are still flashing."

"Put up with it then and stop bombarding me with questions."

Neighing Horse was no longer contrary. Stuffing a corner of the bed clothes in his mouth and closing his eyes, he fell asleep.

Sleep, however, didn't come to Righteous Kindness Zhou, not because of the bandits but because of Sprout.

Sprout and Steamed Bun had become engaged in the spring. Steamed Bun was nineteen and Sprout was sixteen – the same ages as the young sweethearts in the folk song *Third Brother is Nineteen and Fourth Sister is Sixteen*.

In the eyes of the people of Ancestral Worshippers Shrine, when a girl reached sixteen, she was in the prime of her youth. Why? She was both moist and tender. The villagers likened girls to vegetables and fruit. Another saying went: *she is so tender that she'll ooze juice at a pinch*. *Moist* and *tender* were presented as synonymous properties.

Following this adage, Heavenly Music Zhao sought out Righteous Kindness Zhou the cobbler to propose marriage on behalf of Steamed Bun. What is more, according to the saying, he tried to convince the cobbler to allow Steamed Bun and Sprout to tie the knot within the year. Zhou appeared a little unwilling to marry off his daughter. Zhao had repeatedly approached him to talk about this specific matter, but he dodged the issue every time. Heavenly Music

Zhao told Steamed Bun to think about the business between him and Sprout, implying that he should do a little homework on her as a means of talking around her father.

Righteous Kindness Zhou was genuinely reluctant to marry off his daughter. He lost his wife when Sprout was six. He was left a widower and Sprout became a motherless child. Righteous Kindness Zhou originally wanted to get remarried, though he dismissed this thought when he saw how Sprout addressed him as "Pa" with tearful eyes – he was afraid that any stepmother might not treat her well enough. He remained single and served as both a father and a mother until Sprout could sew and darn and wash and brush. Thereafter, he could jettison the typically maternal duties and just be a dad. Sprout knew how to grow up quickly. Both her eyebrows and her figure filled out propitiously and the more she matured, the more delectable she became. With her dexterous hands, she was fond of snipping paper into patterns to make window decorations and enjoyed doing needlework as well. She kept alive the bloodline of her father. When Righteous Kindness Zhou cobbled shoes, she helped by scraping at the soles.

Father and daughter had barely managed to eke out a dignified life full of care and concern. All too soon she had reached marriageable age. The time would soon come when she would move into another household.

Two years earlier, Righteous Kindness Zhou had taken in Neighing Horse as his apprentice. Neighing Horse, bereft of both a home and relatives, had wandered to Ancestral Worshippers Shrine. He was honest and diligent and one year younger than Sprout. His age was immaterial. It transpired that he had a chicken's heart and a speech impediment. Not Zhou's image of a son-in-law.

Sprout had never considered Neighing Horse in that light, being more a brother and a housemate. One day, she was stitching another cloth pouch.

"Oh, oh. Who are you making this sachet for?" Zhou wanted to know.

Sprout removed a string of pouches from the box at the head of her *kang* and arranged them into two lines, saying: "This one is for you and this one is for Neighing Horse."

"I am asking you about the one in your hands?"

"I am going to make a pair of them, but they haven't found a master yet. Whoever gets them will be blessed."

"Oh, oh, have you caught hold of anything the villagers are gossiping about?"

"Father, why are you nagging so much today?"

He no longer pressed her, raising the subject of Steamed Bun instead. "What should I say if Steamed Bun's father comes again to propose marriage?"

"Say whatever you see fit."

"I should say I need to find a well-matched young man for my Sprout."

"You plan to talk like this? He'll follow that up by asking if Steamed Bun is a decent match. What will you say?"

"Steamed Bun has fine features for sure, but his eyes are a little on the small side."

"No, his eyebrows are swarthy and jet black and his eyes look spirited."

"Oh, oh, I should think about it carefully."

Sprout pursed her lips and tossed the sachet aside. "If I do get married, I will marry someone from Ancestral Worshippers Shrine. I won't go looking outside."

It was obvious for whom the sachet was intended. The engagement followed.

On the night of the bandits' arrival, Righteous Kindness Zhou's mind meandered this way and that until he tired himself out. When he was getting ready to fall asleep, a series of knocks on the gate roused him. Someone was pounding at his entrance. Feeling his scalp tightening, he kicked Neighing Horse repeatedly. "Hurry, hurry, Neighing Horse."

Neighing Horse sat up with a start. Righteous Kindness Zhou could hear Sprout thundering her way to open the gate. While shouting out "Ah, ah, ah", Righteous Kindness Zhou flung on his smalls and began to slide down from the *kang*. Sprout had already reached the door before he had time to compose himself.

"It is Brother Steamed Bun," Sprout yelled.

Righteous Kindness Zhou's bubbling adrenaline dispersed in an instant and he leaned against the wall by the *kang* heaving a long sigh.

"Brother Steamed Bun said that he wants to have a word with me."

"Where is he?"

"Here," Steamed Bun answered. "I want to talk with Sprout."

Righteous Kindness Zhou was again filled with adrenaline and sat bolt upright. "Come in."

Steamed Bun and Sprout both entered the room.

"How many times have you slunk to my home when you thought I didn't know?" Righteous Kindness Zhou asked Steamed Bun. "Every time you come, you either ask Sprout to leave the gate open or pry open the bolt like a burglar. Why did you knock at the gate tonight?"

"I jemmied open the bolt again, but a carrying pole was pushed firmly behind it."

"See how you've scared Neighing Horse!"

"No, no, no," the boy apprentice stammered. "I was afraid

that it might be the ban, ban, bandits."

Neighing Horse retreated back under the quilt.

"My father said the bandits will hit the road tomorrow after they have slept overnight in the Heaven and Earth Temple," Steamed Bun related.

"Father," Sprout protested. "You see, there is no stopping you." Tugging at Steamed Bun, Sprout wanted to escort him to her bedroom.

"No," her father insisted. "I still have some questions."

Sprout called out "Father!" once again. Righteous Kindness Zhou had to say: "OK, I'll ask no more. I already know the answers."

Righteous Kindness Zhou retreated back under the quilt while muttering to himself: "Go on chit-chatting. My jaw will stay shut if your marriage is brought up."

Steamed Bun couldn't find much to talk about. So, they exchanged a few words about the bandits. "What do the bandits look like?" Sprout probed.

"Like normal people. They rode on donkeys instead of horses or mules but each rider had a long blade. They have a homemade gun too. Our neighbours were so scared that not a soul could be seen on the street."

"Weren't you scared?"

Steamed Bun thought awhile and then replied: "Yeah."

"You were scared, yet you still went out of the door at so late an hour?"

"I was scared at first, but I calmed down later on. I even went to summon them for the banquet."

"Neighing Horse was so terrified he peed his pants. I worried about you the moment he said there were bandits, but my father wouldn't let me go out." Sprout's eyes were suddenly filled with tears and her fingers pinched at the buttons on Steamed Bun's cloth shirt. "You don't know how worried I was and how my father lectured me."

Steamed Bun grabbed Sprout's waist and exclaimed: "My father lectured me too and told me not to think about the bandits. My father said that after the bandits hit the road, Ancestral Worshippers Shrine would still be Ancestral Worshippers Shrine and he told me to think about the business between me and you. I was at loss, so came here to look for you." Steamed Bun tightened his grip and continued: "When my father came to look for your father, your father struck back. When my father came again, your father struck back again."

Sprout planted her head in Steamed Bun's chest and said: "Just think about it: when I leave, only my father and Neighing Horse will be left behind."

"It is only a matter of time. What do you think about it?"

"Brother Steamed Bun, don't worry. I don't want you to worry and my father knows that it is only a matter of time as well."

Steamed Bun stuck one hand beneath Sprout's clothes. His breath immediately became heavy. Sprout almost shrieked but, afraid that her father might overhear, she bit her lip and remained mute, surrendering herself to Steamed Bun's caresses. The lad grew restless and prepared to unbutton Sprout's clothes. But she shook her head firmly and clasped her hand over his to restrain him.

"Let me take a look. I want to have a look."

Righteous Kindness Zhou coughed once.

Sprout suddenly removed Steamed Bun's hand and raised her voice to say: "Only one is done. Take a good look at them after they are both ready."

Steamed Bun didn't know what had hit him.

Sprout went on in a low voice: "I said that for my father's ears."

Unable to find a spot to rest, Steamed Bun's hands ached with disappointment. Sprout didn't want to upset him and again guided one of his mitts beneath her garments. Steamed Bun started to pinch and fondle again.

"Brother Steamed Bun," Sprout implored. "If you don't leave, my father will never fall asleep."

"Mmm," Steamed Bun murmured. He squeezed and stroked undaunted.

8.

Heavenly Music Zhao rose very early. Steamed Bun's mother fetched him a basinful of water to wash his face. He asked about his son. She replied that he hadn't come back home to sleep until the second half of the night, and wanted to know why Heavenly Music Zhao had raised this.

"No reason." He splashed his face casually a few times, wiped it dry and tossed the towel back into the washbasin.

"No, no, you're not clean yet," his wife remarked and fished out the towel for him to give himself another once over. He tried again and invited her to inspect the results.

"Now am I clean?"

She surveyed his appearance attentively for a minute and then dabbed the corners of his eyes a number of times with the cloth, sighing: "That's better."

"After Steamed Bun gets up," Heavenly Music instructed, "don't let him step foot outdoors but tell him to stay at home and whitewash the walls. As soon as I've seen off the bandits, I'll seek out the shoemaker. He can avoid me on the first day of the month but the fifteenth is going too far."

As he crossed the threshold, he stressed one more time: "Remember: do not go out of this door. There's no use in reinforcing the gate with a carrying pole. The bandits will still storm into any home they please."

Heavenly Music Zhao then trudged to the Heaven and Earth Temple.

It was evident that the bandits were not willing to go on their way. The bedding they had used last night was left in disarray about the courtyard and hadn't been tidied. The dozen or so donkeys were still hitched behind the main hall and had not yet been led out. Something fishy lingered in the air. All along the section of road from the gate of the temple to the main hall, the self-taught marksman and Earthen Jar dogged him like he was a prisoner under escort. After watching him step into the main hall, they again headed back to the temple gate to stand guard. The faces of all the bandits in the courtyard were like shards of raw iron. None of them offered a greeting despite seeing him walking inside. Gone was the conviviality of last night's dining companions.

When Heavenly Music Zhao stepped over the threshold, he thought to himself: "This situation demands extra caution. I should strain every nerve to make sure they speak the language of human beings and don't slip into that outlaw jargon, then see them off without any incident."

From the moment he spotted the bandits, this was his constant line of reasoning. This was a job that demanded patience. He should be patient from the beginning to the end. Every syllable should be imbued with patience.

Ninth Kid and Profound Meditation Wu were sitting on the cloth hassocks used by worshippers to kowtow to the gods with glowing incense sticks in their hands. It was as if they were waiting for him.

Heavenly Music Zhao wanted to loosen up a little. He turned his head to glimpse outside the main hall and remarked: "You've barely woken up. I hurried all the way here expecting you'd risen early."

Profound Meditation Wu drew a hassock over for Heavenly Music Zhao. "Oh, oh," the guest murmured and dropped himself down opposite Ninth Kid.

Ninth Kid massaged his eyes and groaned: "I didn't sleep well. All through the night, my mind was churning. The more my mind churned, the harder it was to fall asleep."

Heavenly Music Zhao also rubbed his eyes and echoed: "I didn't fall asleep until the early hours either. But when I thought that a band of guests at the Heaven and Earth Temple was waiting for me to see them off and that I should get up early the next morning, I forced myself to sleep – not so well, as it happens – and had to wash my face twice. My missus still had to wipe the sleep from the corners of my eyes."

"You see," Ninth Kid whispered to his comrade. "What I have surmised is not wrong."

"Yeah, yeah," Profound Meditation Wu agreed.

Heavenly Music Zhao felt that their words had something to do with him, but they seemed to be putting on a two-man comic show. Unable to understand what they meant, he probed: "You are thinking about me having to wash my face twice after getting up? How not even that was enough to shift the muck from my eyes? That I will never buy."

"No, no. I am thinking that you have mistaken us for beggars," Ninth Kid replied.

"Ah, ah?" Zhao had not thought that Ninth Kid would talk like this. "Never. How could I? From the moment you entered the village – please think back on it – have I mistaken you for beggars? Never, never. Would we lay on a banquet for beggars?"

"You'd throw a banquet to send us packing."

"Send you packing by throwing a banquet? But we've even prepared grain for you."

"Yeah, allow us to dine a little, sup a little and take away a little. After a one-night stand, we'd be off in a hurry and hit the road. That is being *sent packing*."

Heavenly Music's heart contracted. He recalled his words to Steamed Bun the night before. It appeared that the bandits were not wrong to put it this way. His heart contracted even more: The bandits' train of thought should never have been allowed to turn this way.

"Oh, oh, so that's what you're thinking," Zhao mused.

"If not like this, then how?" replied Ninth Kid. "If you and I traded places, what would you think?"

"I would think that we had been welcomed."

"You are welcome. Please dine a little, sup a little and take away a little and then get your arses out of here. That is still being *sent packing*."

"People's kindness should be received in the spirit it is meant. According to your words, it was a mistake to lay on a banquet."

"The mistake wasn't you throwing the banquet but sending us packing. You came to the Heaven and Earth Temple early only in order to send us packing."

"Don't think like that. Have I said anything about sending you packing? Have I said that I am here to send you packing?"

"You haven't used those exact words. You said '*see off*'. It is a subtle change of phrase, like calling a rat a mouse, isn't it?"

"No, I didn't mean that!"

Heavenly Music Zhao was seized with a sudden panic. Impatient and nonplussed, he rose from the hassock and paced to and fro. "I don't know what to say. I don't want to say anything now. I only want to walk out of here. It is really strange that there are people in this world whose minds operate like this."

"Have you ever seen locusts, by any chance?"

"Locusts? No, never. But the older folk once said that wherever locusts pass by, not a blade of grass will be left standing."

"How come you've never seen locusts?"

"Thanks to the Old Lord Heaven and His blessings they have never come here."

"Tell me: where should the locusts go and where should they not go?"

"You got me there. I haven't a clue."

"Old Broke Heaven is unfair. Tell me if Old Broke Heaven is fair or not?"

"You got me again. I've no idea. But why have we rambled onto the subject of locusts?"

"Do you ever think of Old Fourth Ren?"

"No, because he is already dead. My brain has enough to cope with taking care of the living, so I excuse myself from the business of the dead."

"Then think about this: why did Old Fourth Ren die?"

Heavenly Music pondered. When Ninth Kid mentioned Old Fourth Ren, his scalp tightened. He realised that he should be cautious with every word he spoke.

"I've given it some thought. On the face of it, it was a tragic case of human error – someone gunned down with a homemade firearm. But, mulling it over again, this was a disaster ordained by the Old Lord Heaven. The lifespan bestowed upon this man had run its course. Therefore, He changed him into a Mongolian gazelle at that very moment and let him gambol right into the line of fire."

"You don't want to gambol right into the line of fire of a homemade gun, do you?"

"I don't."

"What about onto the end of a blade?"

"No. They're both deadly weapons."

"I want to order our gang to set down roots in Ancestral Worshippers Shrine. You are the Village Head – what do you think about it?"

"Set down roots here?"

"Think about how to transplant a tree. You move a tree from somewhere else, plant it and then water it regularly. *Transplant a tree.* Do you know what I am talking about?"

Heavenly Music Zhao was silent.

"If you think this is too daunting, raise a few bushels of grain for us first. That isn't difficult, is it?"

"If you say this is difficult, it is not. But if you say it is not difficult, it is. That depends on how you think about it. I mean, what do you mean by the word 'first'?"

"I mean that the grain should be raised for starters and then we can talk about transplanting the tree."

"Oh, oh." Heavenly Music left the temple with Ninth Kid staring at him.

Earthen Jar ran into the main hall: "Why has he gone so soon? To fetch us some wine and rice?"

His heart unsteady, Ninth Kid paid no attention to Earthen Jar. "What do you think about it?" he quizzed Profound Meditation Wu.

"The way I see it, it's less than ideal."

"Then we should kill someone."

Ninth Kid raised his head to look at Earthen Jar.

"Don't glare at me," Earthen Jar yelped. "It seems like you are raring to do me in."

"I won't kill you. But I will permit you to kill. Is that OK?"

"You won't? You won't?"

Ninth Kid wanted to study the brown paper. Earthen Jar took it out while saying: "You looked at it already last night and now you want to look at it again?"

As he scanned the brown paper, Ninth Kid asked: "Do you miss our village?"

"Yeah, but if I'm honest I miss my wife more."

"Just by following these markings on the brown paper, could you find your way back home?"

"I could even without looking at them. You were talking about *killing someone* a moment ago but now you're on about *going back to our home village*."

"It's the same thing."

"I don't understand."

"The Village Head has gone to gather grain. After the grain has been gathered, you carry it back to our home village and take the opportunity to look in on your wife as well as the other folks' wives. If they don't gather the grain, then you must kill someone for us. Then they will have to hand it over and it can be sent back to our home village. Now do you understand?"

"Will we kill the Village Head?"

"Maybe yes, maybe no. It depends."

Earthen Jar whipped out his blade from its scabbard and took a look at it: "With this?"

"Don't talk nonsense."

"I am afraid that I can't be that hardhearted. The Village Head gave us a feast with meat and wine. He is a decent sort."

"If he can't gather up that grain, he is not a decent sort."

"Don't go to the courtyard. Drop in at the village to see which way the wind is blowing," ordered Ninth Kid.

Earthen Jar immediately tensed up: "Should I go there alone?"

"Take the hare hunter with you."

"I could go there on my own. Then again, there is strength in numbers."

Earthen Jar and the marksman soon came back.

"There's not so much as a dog-sized dwarf out on the village street," Earthen Jar reported. "The Village Head wasn't gathering grain at all. Instead, he was brushing the walls at home, making ready for his son's marriage!"

"True or false?" asked Ninth Kid.

"I went over there to check it out. He and his son were tempering the walls. Each had a basin full of muddy water and a mop. Bloodlust practically surged out of my gallbladder but I thought that it would be better to come back first and fill you in."

"I will go over there to have a look," Ninth Kid said to Profound Meditation Wu.

A little worried, Wu asked Ninth Kid: "Can you make it happen?"

"Humans are not mindless locusts."

Earthen Jar was not lying. Heavenly Music Zhao and Steamed Bun were brushing the walls of one of their rooms by dipping mops into muddy water. The distemper was made by mixing fine dirt and water together. After being slathered with it, the walls became smooth and glossy.

Barely had Ninth Kid and his gang reached the gate when Steamed Bun's mother was seized with terror. "They are coming; they are coming and they've got one more bloke this time. What should we do?"

"Go to the main room to take care of the old folks," instructed Heavenly Music. Steamed Bun's mother duly went to the main room.

Ninth Kid and his gang reached the door.

"You see," said Earthen Jar. "We have come along but they are still brushing away as if nothing has happened."

Ninth Kid watched them coat the wall and then told Steamed Bun to make himself scarce.

"Since you've been instructed to get out, do as you're told," Zhao insisted.

Steamed Bun went out to the courtyard.

"I am taking care of the wall, but it won't hinder our conversation."

"Suit yourself," responded Ninth Kid. "Nobody is stopping you, but you haven't gathered the grain. You haven't given it a second thought."

"I have. I have thought about it until my head aches. I have weighed it over and over and finally concluded that you should just leave. Ancestral Worshippers Shrine needs to go back to normal."

"Oh, oh." Ninth Kid was deliberately inarticulate. He nodded his head several times and then opened his mouth again.

"Our talk at the temple was a waste of time. You haven't taken in even one word."

"I can't."

"Why?"

Heavenly Music Zhao no longer plied his brush but turned to face Ninth Kid.

"Because you didn't talk to me seriously. Because you talked in the language of bandits."

Ninth Kid, also focusing on Heavenly Music Zhao, seemingly flashed him a smile. Heavenly Music Zhao turned back to attend to the wall again.

"You can't be the Village Head any longer."

"Why?"

"You won't follow my instructions. I'll replace you with someone who does."

Heavenly Music Zhao spun around: "You? You replace me?"

"Yeah, I shall transform you."

"Shouldn't the villagers be the ones to replace their head man?"

"I will see to it."

Heavenly Music Zhao smiled. "Then it will be me again. If you don't believe me, just try it."

He resumed brushing the wall.

"Can the people have a dead man as their Village Head?"

"I am not dead yet. Old Lord Heaven has the say-so over life and death."

"Whether other people live or die is decided by Old Broke Heaven's say-so, but I decide whether you live or die."

Heavenly Music Zhao turned round once more; this time he did it especially quickly and with a *whoosh*. The homemade gun was already in the hands of Ninth Kid. Zhao froze and opened his eyes wide. Tawny-coloured water was dripping down to the floor from the doused mop in his hand. His legs were bowing and shaking.

"Don't, don't. I will talk with them about the grain …"

"Too late."

Ninth Kid raised his hand and hooked his finger on the trigger. Bang! Heavenly Music Zhao's face was gone.

His body pitched forward before thumping heavily back against the wall behind him. He bucked a couple times, slid down and lay doubled up on the floor. The doused mop in his hand hadn't been catapulted away by the shock. It remained gripped fast, plopping still in his hand into the basin full of muddy water beside him.

On hearing gunshot, Steamed Bun shouted "Father" and staggered back towards the room. Before he could catch sight of him, he was kicked to his knees outside the door. His arms were wrestled behind his back by the shooter and Earthen Jar, who also gripped his hair. Steamed Bun cried: "I want to see my father!"

In just a few strides, Ninth Kid reached Steamed Bun,

crammed the mouth of the barrel of the homemade gun into his mouth and snarled at the mother, grandfather and grandmother who were emerging from the main room, crying and shouting: "Don't move!"

They immediately gagged their mouths and were still.

Saliva slithered from Steamed Bun's lips as they were prized apart by the homemade gun.

"Tell all your neighbours to go to the village office," Ninth Kid commanded Steamed Bun. "Tell all the men to get over there. You hear me?"

"Yes, yes," his mother wailed. "Steamed Bun, you did hear him!"

"You hear me?"

Steamed Bun nodded his head firmly again and again.

"That's good." The bandit leader withdrew the rifle. "Release him and let him see his father," he instructed Earthen Jar and the marksman.

Steamed Bun didn't get up. With his head wrapped in his arms, he curled up and wailed inconsolably.

9.

"Father, how can you still sit tight?" Sprout yelled. "Steamed Bun's father has been killed by the bandits and you just sit there." Sprout stamped her foot. She had done it repeatedly.

Righteous Kindness Zhou was stitching the sole to the upper of a shoe. Neighing Horse was sewing a sole. They each picked up a pair of top plates and sat side by side in the courtyard.

"Say something, Father!"

Righteous Kindness Zhou made no sound. After finishing the shoe, he removed it from the top plates and severed the string with scissors. He then took the shoe in his hand and studied it from the front and rear and left and right before standing up and retreating to his bedchamber.

Sprout wiped away her tears with the back of her hand.

"Don't, *en, ai*, cry," Neighing Horse tried to reassure her.

Sprout turned her back on him and cried out.

Righteous Kindness Zhou returned with another shoe and put it right next to the newly-made one to be observed and matched. The shoes were of a piece. Whenever a pair of shoes was finished, he would put them together to inspect – to check them out as well as to appreciate.

"She is crying," Neighing Horse noted. "You see."

"The lasts," Righteous Kindness requested.

Neighing Horse rose to his feet after an "Oh" and swiftly fetched the wooden box that was used to store the lasts. Righteous Kindness Zhou chose two from a series of suitable ones, stuffed them into the shoes and pounded them solid.

The shoes immediately became spirited and lively and bulged out taut. He put them side by side on the windowsill.

Zhou tugged at Sprout's arm. "Don't cry, don't cry."

Sprout lurched sideways and cried more violently. She seemed to have endless tears to be dabbed away.

"Sprout doesn't want to talk to her father, does she?" Righteous Kindness Zhou said and pulled at Sprout's arm again. "Stop crying. OK?"

Sprout recoiled and continued sobbing.

Righteous Kindness Zhou no longer bothered Sprout's arm. "You don't want to talk to your father. Then your father has no options left. Just keep on crying."

"You refuse to talk to me!" cried Sprout.

She wept again.

"I can talk, I can talk. Just now I was busy stitching the sole to the shoe and finishing the last few stitches. Now I am all ears."

"I asked you to go to Steamed Bun's home with me and you refused. I said I would go alone but you didn't let me."

"Brother Steamed Bun is now just Steamed Bun."

"If I call him Brother Steamed Bun you just laugh at me. Will you accompany me or not?"

"I shall not."

"I shall!"

"I mean I shall not go over there *now*. Do you want to know why?"

"Why?"

"Do you know what the precise situation is at Steamed Bun's home at the moment? Can you be sure the bandits won't darken his door again? Steamed Bun is young and headstrong. The bandits killed his father. Will he stick his neck out to fight back with a cleaver? Steamed Bun and the bandits are dicing with death but you and I are on the sidelines. Should we run away and hide or give him a helping hand? If we hide or run away, we will be a laughing stock for the rest of our lives. If we help Steamed Bun fight the bandits, we can never hope to prevail. Bandits are bandits, but we are people. How can people defeat bandits? If we push our luck to fight them, we know that we can't win. We'll surely end up being slain. What if the bandits swoop on them again? You haven't even thought this through but you want to go to Steamed Bun's home. Steamed Bun, Steamed Bun, Steamed Bun. How can you go over there? What do you expect to happen? How do you know that the bandits will no longer bother them?"

Righteous Kindness switched to the topic of the nuptials between Sprout and Steamed Bun. "It feels neither kind nor chivalrous to talk about this at the time when disaster has just struck Steamed Bun's family. That young man speaks, swaggers and does everything confidently. Half of his confidence stemmed from his father and his status as Village Head. Though he might still be confident, he can't be as confident anymore. The situation has changed. His father's dead and his prop is gone."

Sprout shouted: "Father!"

"Alright, alright, as you don't like it, I'll no longer gabble away. I will ask you one more question. Alright?"

"What question?"

"You've no need to answer me right away. Just answer me when you have thought it over. If Steamed Bun were no longer the Steamed Bun he used to be, would you – I am asking you now – would you still marry him?"

"I would."

"Why?"

"You have asked me more than one question."

"Then I will ask you another one. You must have answered me too hastily."

"You are rubbing salt into someone else's wound, Father."

"Rubbing salt? You have thought yourself into salt? You are salt then?"

"If someone were at the bottom of the well, I wouldn't ever be the one to fling a stone down there."

"But you shouldn't jump down the well after him either, Sprout."

"I would jump down. I have my eye on him. I don't want to talk with you anymore."

"Stop talking, stop talking. These are only some idle questions. Just imagine: the bandits are still at large. Something's bound to happen, right? If Steamed Bun has gone to the Heaven and Earth Temple to look for the bandits – just imagine. Are we still speaking hypothetically?"

Bang, bang, bang – there was a knock on the gate.

Neighing Horse's legs seized up in fear.

"Quick," Righteous Kindness Zhou cried and pushed Sprout towards her room.

It was Steamed Bun. Steamed Bun hammered at the gate a few more times, shouting: "Uncle Shoemaker, it is me."

"Brother Steamed Bun! It is Brother Steamed Bun." Squawking like a magpie, Sprout opened the gate and invited Steamed Bun to come in.

Steamed Bun didn't enter. His head was wrapped in a piece of mourning cloth. His face had the texture of frost-bitten leaves.

"Uncle Shoemaker. The bandits have instructed all the men in the village to go to the village office to elect a Village Head after the meal."

Steamed Bun's voice sounded frostbitten as well.

"Brother Steamed Bun. Step in. Step in and talk."

"I can't go through a neighbour's gate wearing a mourning headdress," Steamed Bun declined.

Sprout yanked the cloth wrapping from Steamed Bun's crown in one go. "Now you can and this is not just a neighbour's compound. Step in. I am inviting you to step in."

"There are still a few households I haven't relayed the news to yet."

"You don't have to relay the news yet. You can do it in a little while," Sprout protested, dragging him inside the gate.

The frostbitten Steamed Bun ducked his head.

Tears suddenly flooded out of Sprout's eyes.

"Brother Steamed Bun."

She patted away the tracks of her tears with both hands.

"Doh, doh, don't cry," consoled Neighing Horse.

"Come a little further inside," beckoned Righteous Kindness Zhou. "Only one small gate separates us from the world out there and anyone could be eavesdropping."

Sprout made simple work of drawing Steamed Bun into her room. "It is best to go in there," said Righteous Kindness Zhou. "It is safer." He then stood outside listening to the exchange between Sprout and Steamed Bun.

"Brother Steamed Bun. I wanted to come over to see you." He shook his head. "What is wrong with your mouth? Your heart's so bitter that you've chewed your lip bloody."

Steamed Bun shook his head, explaining: "They stabbed at me with the rifle. They gripped my head, wrestled my arms back and crammed the barrel in my mouth, forcing me to stay still." He sobbed. "After they had a few words with my father, they fired. My father's face was shot to smithereens." He squatted down and clasped his hands over his nose and mouth, stifling his crying. "They told my father to gather grain for them. My father was reluctant at first but willing to do that later. They said *it was too late* and fired at him. Barely had I chance to call out 'Father' when they crammed that thing into my mouth. I felt so suffocated and abused. I want to find somewhere to cry my eyes out because I daren't do that at home. My mother has cried herself unconscious more than once and then there is my grandpa and my grandma. Whatever should I do?"

Sprout gripped Steamed Bun's arm and persuaded him not to cry by adding "Brother Steamed Bun" to everything she said. She enjoined and enjoined but sobbed herself.

Zhou and Neighing Horse's eyes were wet too. "Sprout," Zhou counselled. "Let Steamed Bun cry out. There is so much anguish in there."

Sprout was loath to let him to continue on his rounds. She wanted to metamorphose herself into something – something soft and warm that could enfold Steamed Bun within. She believed that she could as long as she was willing to. She told Steamed Bun to come to her place that night. "Brother Steamed Bun, come to me again tonight," she rasped.

Righteous Kindness Zhou handed the pair of new shoes on the windowsill to Steamed Bun. "Your father told me to make them in better times. They are just finished. The lasts are still inside. Remove them before you slip the shoes on your father's feet. I won't charge for them. Take them as a gift from me to your father. Let your father leave this world in new footwear." He also commiserated with Steamed Bun: "No Village Head will be elected. Nobody could take your father's place. Besides, nobody at Ancestral Worshippers Shrine will lay aside their conscience and want to be Village Head. If you don't believe me, just wait and see."

Steamed Bun departed. Sprout asked her father whether he planned to go to the village office.

"I shall. Both Neighing Horse and I will. Nobody dares refuse. If you don't believe me, just wait and see. The bandits will visit anyone who stays at home."

10.

All the men of Ancestral Worshippers Shrine went to the village office. Seventy or eighty of them squatted down in the courtyard. The gongs, drums and other musical instruments and willow wood legs used yesterday were strewn incongruously about the steps as if they had nothing to do with the occupants of the courtyard.

Steamed Bun was present too. He crouched among the crowd with his head wrapped in the mourning headdress buried in the crook of his arms.

Not all the bandits were there. Ninth Kid left two of them behind at the Heaven and Earth Temple to build a kitchen.

The Village Head was elected by drawing lots. "When I told you to nominate somebody, no one spoke up," Ninth Kid intoned. "If I were to appoint a Head, I am afraid that he might not be suitable. Then let's draw lots. Whoever wins will become the Village Head, fair and square. The Village Head will be your spokesman. Everyone among you is eligible for the position."

The self-taught marksman stood in front of Ninth Kid, holding the loaded rifle. The others stood separately with their swords. They didn't feel nervous because Ninth Kid had announced a supplementary item of discipline: "You can squat down or sit down – just don't stand up. Whoever stands up is ready to forfeit his life." Hence, they only needed to be primed if someone got ready to stand up.

Earthen Jar and Profound Meditation Wu were scrunching paper into balls in one room. A cymbal that Earthen Jar had conveniently picked up from the steps was on the table. After they had reduced a slip of paper into a ball, they tossed it into the concave centre of the upturned disc. While doing this, Earthen Jar exclaimed to Profound Meditation Wu: "We killed others before – that was done accidentally when we were taken unawares. But not this time. We were chatting amiably. The chief took over the homemade gun, said 'too late', raised his hand and hooked his finger on the trigger. *Bang*, the Village Head's face was completely ripped off. Bravo, bravo! I was waiting for the chief to say the word when *hei*, he had done it himself. *Bang*."

Only one small slip of paper was left. Earthen Jar raised it, mumbling to the paper as if it could hear: "So, whoever picks you is the Village Head." He used the inked end of a small bamboo tube to leave a red circle on it and then blew on it to dry it before mixing the lots in the cymbal. When he lifted the receptacle, he mused: "How nice it would be if the emperor were elected this way. I'll risk my arm and draw one too. Try my luck."

Earthen Jar was holding the instrument in his hands as he stood in front of Ninth Kid. "The slips of paper have been balled up according to the head count," he informed him. "Not one more and not one less."

"Let them draw lots."

Earthen Jar instructed the villagers to select a ball one by one. "One lot per person. Get a move on and unroll the paper after you have drawn. If you see a red circle, speak up. The one who does will be the Village Head."

In the courtyard, the sound of balled-up paper being snatched could be heard. Gasps were audible too – as they drew lots, everyone held their breath, only letting it free when they found out there was no red circle.

Steamed Bun drew his lot. There was no red circle on it. He too heaved a long sigh of relief and threw the paper at his feet. "Don't toss it away, don't toss it away," scolded Earthen Jar. "If you treat it as trash, things will get messed up." He retrieved it.

Righteous Kindness Zhou didn't allow Neighing Horse to draw a lot. He reasoned that Neighing Horse was still a juvenile. "Draw one," Earthen Jar demanded. "If he doesn't draw, one ball will be left behind. What would we do if it was the one with the red circle?" Neighing Horse then obeyed.

Righteous Kindness Zhou took his turn. When he was getting ready to unroll the papery pellet, Neighing Horse cried out: "No, no, no, no!"

"What's wrong? What's wrong?" Zhou enquired.

His mouth twitching, Neighing Horse told Righteous Kindness to look at what he had unfolded. Earthen Jar turned round, snatching it away in a flash. He studied it carefully, then stared intently at Neighing Horse.

"How come you drew the lucky lot? Tell me."

There was no need for the others to try their hand and so all of them heaved a long sigh of relief.

Neighing Horse's face was already convulsed out of shape. "No, no, no, no!"

Ninth Kid came over and took up the lot to examine it.

Worry-stricken, Righteous Kindness Zhou wanted to stand up and speak but Earthen Jar kicked him flat on the floor.

"Yeah, that's the one," Earthen Jar said to Ninth Kid. "I pressed the red circle on it."

Righteous Kindness Zhou, who had been kicked so that he landed on all fours, protested: "He can't, he can't be the Village Head."

Ninth Kid peered at Righteous Kindness Zhou, demanding: "How do you know he can't?"

"He is only fifteen and stammers. He is not a local lad but an apprentice of mine."

"Then you take his place and be the Village Head."

Taken aback, Righteous Kindness Zhou fixed Ninth Kid with anxious eyeballs. He sat rooted on the ground.

Neighing Horse got ready to cry. "No, no, no, no!"

Earthen Jar raised the cymbal, aimed it at Neighing Horse's head and rammed it onto him like a cap. Letting out a cry, Neighing Horse collapsed against his master's chest.

"You have a new Village Head now," Ninth Kid announced to all the others in the courtyard.

The remaining villagers rose to their feet and slunk out silently one after another.

"The Village Head will be around to raise grain early tomorrow morning," Earthen Jar declared. "One bushel per household."

Profound Meditation Wu blinked his tiny eyes rapidly and walked over to Ninth Kid. "You are right. Men are not locusts. No matter how huge the crowd is, they are still individuals out for themselves."

"Don't leave!" Righteous Kindness suddenly yelled out. "I can't replace Neighing Horse. Neighing Horse can't be the Village Head. You can't leave!"

Having apparently not heard his protests, the other villagers left Righteous Kindness Zhou and Neighing Horse there.

"I can't be the Village Head," Zhou pleaded with Ninth Kid.

The marksman sneaked a glimpse at Ninth Kid and suddenly reached out the firearm to butt Righteous Kindness on the forehead.

"Now can you?"

II.

The moment Righteous Kindness Zhou reached home the next evening, he asked Sprout if she had warmed the water in the sun for him. Sprout replied that a large tub was ready. Righteous Kindness Zhou told Neighing Horse to help him carry the basin to the rear of his compound. "Neighing Horse," he instructed. "Go and fetch a horse ladle. I need to give my body a decent rinse. That damned grain may taste good, but it's a dirty business to put it away. Add some sweat into the mix and it is sticky and smells foul." He stripped himself naked, sat in the tub and requested that Neighing Horse scrub him down. Then he stood up and asked the boy to pour water over him with the horse ladle. "Do it inch by inch from my head down," he instructed. After Neighing Horse poured one ladleful of water, he cried out: "So comfortable, so comfortable." His spirits raised, the lad wanted to carry on pouring water like this for all eternity.

"*Shifu* – master," he began. "The moment you stepped out of the door with the bandits, I was afraid that you wouldn't make it through the day."

"There is no Fire Mountain that can't be crossed," Righteous Kindness Zhou said. "In future I want to have water poured on my body like this every day."

"What about on cloudy and rainy days?"

"After the clouds drift away and the rain has fallen, the sun will come out. Then get the water warm and pour it out. Oh, so comfortable."

Thereafter, he ordered Sprout to fetch a basin of water to scrub behind his ears and even in his ear canals. Next he settled down on the bench he used when making shoes and began an audience with his daughter. "Now I feel fresh and cool in both my body and mind and I want to talk with you."

Zhou began his narrative:

"Steamed Bun was standing right in front of the bandits when they shot his father dead, but what did he do? What did he do apart from acting terrified? His father was shot dead by the bandits and he told the others to go to the village office to elect a Village Head to replace his father. True enough, the bandits forced his hand. And what about me? Did I vie against the others to be the Village Head? I took the post of Village Head for exactly the same reason he informed the others to come to the village office. We are both the same height. He is no more noble in character than me. Sometimes he does seem less lofty though. He has never thought to thank Neighing Horse and me. What if he drew the lot? If he drew the lot, he would have to take his father's place and raise the grain for the bandits. His father is still at his home and has not been laid to rest yet. What would he feel like if he were on the street raising grain for the very same bandits who murdered his father? Why doesn't he think like this?

"Just because my words are unpleasant on the ears, don't loathe them. I haven't said that he is not decent enough. I mean that he is no better than me. When I went to his home to raise the grain, he spat out a mouthful of saliva – to one side, of course – but I knew that he was spitting at me. I gave him a piece of my mind. I said: 'Steamed Bun, behave yourself. My Sprout loves you with a blind affection. For that reason alone you shouldn't have spat in my direction like our neighbours did.' I continued: 'Spittle can send me on my way but not the bandits.' I asked him: 'Aren't you afraid of that homemade gun? I am collecting the grain so that nobody else will die. If I don't, somebody's blood will be shed – most probably yours.' 'Why wouldn't it be yours?' he flashed back. I answered that I had handed in my grain and didn't spit.

"We didn't go into the business of that pair of shoes. I was afraid that talking about it might cause him trouble – two bandits were standing nearby. His father placed an order for them – early too, mind – and I was late getting around to making them. I didn't do that on purpose. Many people call on me to make them shoes and it's usually a matter of first come, first served. When his father died, I thought I should get a move on and finish making them so that he could be buried with a new pair on his feet. I didn't charge him. It was a gift. Steamed Bun didn't want them. He had brought them back home but didn't want them. He was humiliating me with the shoes. His father ordered them. How could he not take them? If the shoes were to be rejected, that should be on his father's say so. He didn't want them and then that was it? Where was my pay? If he is so ambitious, he should give me what I'm owed. Sprout, do you know how your father felt when those shoes were flung in front of him? Your father's heart was almost rotten. I thought: 'Pronto, pronto. Some dog please dash over and scurry off with them between your teeth.' But no dog came. The mutts of our village were also afraid of the bandits. That marksman just tucked the shoes under his waistband."

Apropos the post of Village Head, Righteous Kindness made the following remarks:

"Heavenly Music Zhao was the Village Head, but the bandits didn't allow him to retain the post and shot him dead. You think that he died because he wasn't afraid of the bandits? No. I was standing outside eavesdropping when Steamed Bun related what happened to you. It was too late for his father to feel terror. That he didn't feel terrified sooner brought out the bandits' loathing. The bandits not only require people to be afraid of them but also to be afraid in a timely manner. Had Zhao said that he would raise the grain earlier, he would not be dead and would still be the Village Head. I was afraid that the bandits might use the gun to peel off my face too."

He also passed comment on his fellow villagers:

"Like me, they are all afraid of having to taste the bandits' gun and blades. Otherwise, why did they all file to the village office in such an obedient way? Why did they all hand in the grain so submissively? They took out their anger towards the bandits on me. They chose the wrong guy. Bastards — they have never considered when I said, 'I won't be the Village Head, I will never be the Village Head even if it means being shot to death,' I would have been like Heavenly Music Zhao, entering eternal glory after a single bang. I carried all of this on my back. None of our bastard neighbours said one word out of concern but looked at me with altered eyes; some even spat at me. Just spit at yourselves!"

Righteous Kindness Zhou then asked Sprout: "Are your father's words right?"

"Right but, again, not right."

"What do you mean?"

"Your words sound right, but when I ponder over them, I feel something is amiss. Still, I can't iron my thoughts out. My heart's aflutter now. I can't listen to you anymore."

"I am through with this as well. You think about what's been said carefully and slowly."

12.

Earthen Jar and the self-taught marksman also gave their bodies a rinse. They stripped naked in the temple and used cool water. The grain having been raised, the other rapturous bandits turned the duo's bathtime into a slapstick affair. They surrounded them and used horse ladles for pouring or else made light work of it by dousing their comrades from the head down with buckets of water.

Earthen Jar and the shooter didn't say: "So comfortable." They gasped: "Great shit, great shit – *pooh, pooh!*"

"Earthen Jar, you don't have a stitch on," one bandit teased. "Think of your wife and let your big bull stand up for us to have a look."

"It's been out of service for a long time. A rusty bull now," another commented. "Not only can't it stand up, but it's shrunk. You guys, see."

"It is cool water," Earthen Jar snapped. "Fetch hot water and see if it will stand tall or not. *Pooh, pooh.*"

They quietened down after supper. Sitting in the courtyard, the band listened to the arrangements Ninth Kid had made for Earthen Jar to return to their home village with the grain. He also seconded a bandit by the name of Third Matcher to accompany him. As the self-taught marksman didn't hail from their village, he stood guard outside the temple.

"We have trudged so far and at long last arrived at a fine place," Ninth Kid reflected. "Everything that should be had is to be had here – there are mountains, water and grain; there are no locusts and no droughts. We will sit tight. Every year we will take turns to send grain back to our home village and pay a visit to our kin. Why should Earthen Jar be the first one to go back? Well, on our way here he threw his mind into memorising the map and this might be regarded as rewarding him with a plum job. Third Matcher can be seen as riding on his coat tails. Whoever wants to send word back home should tell Earthen Jar before bedtime. They will hit the road by daybreak."

Earthen Jar immediately became the man of the moment. The company crowded around him with their messages. He listened to them one after another.

"You keep squawking away nonstop. It is too messy and I can't commit your words to memory," he complained. "I will just pick out scraps of information that can be brought up when I get back home."

"Good," they agreed. "Do it."

Earthen Jar condensed their words into three truisms: "When I see your woman, I will say your prick is missing her; when I see your kids, I will say their father wants them to be good children and follow their mother's words; when I see your old people, I will say your son is in clover so there's no need to worry – you see, hasn't he sent you grain."

They all concluded that Earthen Jar had done a commendable job and clapped.

"Applaud my prick," Earthen Jar grumbled. "My heart is at sixes and sevens. I am allowed to sleep at home for only one night. I said: 'It is never easy to go back home. Please allow me to stay there for two more days. I am begging you.' But our chief snapped: 'If you keep on like this, you will be replaced with someone else.' You guys be the judge. Should my heart be at sixes and sevens or not?"

"One night is good enough," another bandit growled.

"The moment you get inside your gate, you'll drag your wife to the brick bed and never get down."

"That is not sensible," someone else moaned. "How can he relay our messages if his legs are weak?"

The others thought there was a point behind the second bandit's words and chimed in: "Yeah, yeah, we should also give Earthen Jar some straightforward advice: first pass on the news and then bunk up."

That night, none of the bandits slept well. All were pining for their village; some were so homesick their eyes became dewy and they kept sniffing.

It was Profound Meditation Wu's idea that Earthen Jar and Third Matcher should embark before dawn. He reasoned that the full glare of day was too eye-prickling to drive four donkeys loaded with grain at a fair lick. Ninth Kid hissed: "Everything was above board about how the grain was raised. Why should we operate on the sly like thieves?"

"We have almost, but not quite, managed to settle here. We should still be mindful of what's going through the locals' minds," Profound Meditation Wu explained. "People are not locusts. You are right on that score. But if we want to stick around here forever we should be vigilant. They might remain passive and never vex us like the locusts did. On the other hand, our greatest concern must be that they are never goaded into swarming."

When he saw off Earthen Jar and Third Matcher, Ninth Kid said: "Let's make one thing perfectly clear: you should protect the grain with your lives."

"Rest assured," Earthen Jar vowed. "As long as we survive, the grain will be with us."

"And what if you don't make it?"

"How could that happen?" Earthen Jar asked. "If I bump

into a robber, I will –" Earthen Jar whipped out his sword and sliced through the air. "There are two of us. Should we run into a thug who we can't tackle, one of us will try to keep him occupied and the other will drive the donkeys to safety. Or what say we sleep in the daytime but rush on our way at night? Either way, the grain will get back home."

"The donkeys should be fed well. You have taken four animals and will come back with four," Ninth Kid added.

"Certainly, certainly."

Ninth Kid stroked the bottom of one beast with an air of attachment. "Hit the road, hit the road," he said. "You son of a jackass, you've got a plum job. If I were not the chief, I'd have been the one who did this."

That day, Old Fourth Ren and Heavenly Music Zhao were interred and met their eternal rest.

Also, from that day the villagers no longer fastened their gates in the daytime. They visited each other. A number also headed to their fields to inspect their crops. Nowhere seemed out of bounds except for the Heaven and Earth Temple.

Profound Meditation Wu commented to Ninth Kid: "Seemingly our first step has been made very steady."

"Then we must think of how to take the second one."

A knot of bandits went into the village to cadge tobacco.

Profound Meditation Wu requested that Ninth Kid announce a further item of discipline: "Nobody should hang about the village too much. Anyone who goes there should avoid letting their mask slip. We are bandits first and last – the locals mustn't know that we once farmed and chopped wood as they do."

13.

On the surface, everyone was living a proper, decent life. Even Old Fourth Ren and Heavenly Music Zhao lay underground in a proper way. Everyone had something decent and proper to hold onto except for Righteous Kindness Zhou.

He was out of work.

For a number of days, no one sought him out to make shoes. Nobody came to collect finished orders. That didn't matter. Neighing Horse was dispatched to pay home visits. The apprentice came back with a wad of money and the ordered shoes. They all claimed that they didn't want the footwear but they would still cover the cost as if in tacit agreement. Further ear-prickling words were to be heard: the shoemaker should send his merchandise to the bandits.

Whatever did they mean? They had paid in full and the footwear belonged to them. Send them to the bandits? They wouldn't do that in person so why were they requesting that he should do it? His neighbours were bullying and humiliating him in broad daylight.

A dozen or more pairs of new shoes were set out in the courtyard. It was as though Righteous Kindness Zhou was not gazing at them but the other way round. An ache took hold in his chest.

Zhou wanted to slap them in the face with the shoes. He wanted to stand on the street and blindly hurl abuse. While screaming bile, he would carelessly fling the shoes one by one onto the rooftop or the dunghill of any household; even if the shoes got tangled in the trees, no matter. They didn't want the shoes? He didn't want them either.

Sprout and Neighing Horse suffered collateral damage from this indignity.

"What should we do?" Sprout wailed. "Nobody wants to talk to us. How can we go on living like this?"

Neighing Horse again said that he wanted to chop off his hand. "This is what's to blame – it chose the lot," he complained. "*Shifu*," he went on. "You go to the street to curse them and I am with you."

Righteous Kindness Zhou neither shouted abuse on the street nor threw away the shoes. "Why should I browbeat them? If I do that, it will be a waste of energy and saliva. So hateful! Why should I throw away the shoes? I made them all, day after day, night after night and stitch after stitch. Why should I throw them away? I won't. I shall keep them for my own use. Neighing Horse, you can help me. I'll wear those big ones, you put on those small ones and Sprout will wear the women's ones."

"I won't," Sprout replied.

Her father took off one of his shoes, slipped his foot casually into a new one and then stamped to and fro about the courtyard while saying to her: "Sprout, you see, you see, you see ..."

His voice grew lower and lower and his paces slower and slower. Finally, he thudded down on the ground and clasped his hands over his face, mute.

Sprout sidled to her room.

Neighing Horse didn't know what to do. He wanted to haul his *shifu* to his feet. His body swaying a few times, he didn't edge forward but stood frozen to the spot. Not until he spotted Ninth Kid and the marksman did he try to screech, "*Shi, shi, shifu*, they are co, co, coming," and gathered the shoes from the ground.

Mr Zhou didn't rise to his feet but stared at Ninth Kid and his henchman. The latter had a donkey in tow with a sack of grain on its back.

"What's up? There's a problem with the grain?"

"No, no, every last grain is good," Ninth Kid answered.

"Then what?"

"We are giving some back to you. You must have tired yourself out and suffered much grief in the process."

"There is no need, there is no need. Everyone should be treated equally without preference. What's more, I haven't suffered any grief and I haven't felt aggrieved either."

"Then this is a reward for you."

The marksman offloaded the grain from the back of the donkey and carried the sack to the steps.

"Guests have crossed your threshold, but you still sit on the ground?"

"My waist aches."

"If your waist is uncomfortable, sitting tight on the ground will make it worse. Stand up and stretch yourself a few times."

"My head is sore as well. I can't sit tight or stand up. I was thinking that I should go to my brick bed and lie down there awhile."

"Oh, oh, I've only got a few words to say. After I've told you my business, you can take a rest."

"More business? Hasn't the grain been raised already? There's more business?"

Righteous Kindness Zhou sprang to his feet.

"This is for the good of the village as well," the outlaw insisted. "We can't go on occupying the Heaven and Earth Temple forever. The temple is where the villagers offer sacrifices to the Heavens, the Earth and the gods. It is not good if we board there and change it into a den for eating, drinking, shitting and pissing – it is an affront to the gods. What's more, the halls are too small and a dozen or so guys can't squeeze in. We could take shelter in the village office, but the village office is down here. My men are all very red-blooded chaps and I can't guarantee that none of them will creep under some neighbour's quilt. That would cause you no end of trouble. What do you say?"

Righteous Kindness Zhou pinched his sideburns with his thumb time and again.

"If your head is really sore, you can sit down on the ground and talk."

"It doesn't ache now. It's spinning instead."

"Tell your apprentice to hold you steady."

Neighing Horse came over hurriedly and shored up Righteous Kindness Zhou.

"I don't know where I should allow you to settle down," the cobbler mused. "I am feeling woozy and my mind can't function properly."

"There is no need for you to wrack your brains. The mountains have so many trees and it is very easy to build a compound full of buildings. I have got my eye on a plot – Old Fourth Ren's winnowing ground is promising. It is not too far from the village and not too near either. You can consult your neighbours and decide who should cut down the trees and who should make the clay bricks. Many hands make light work."

Righteous Kindness Zhou again slapped his forehead with his palm.

"I am through," said Ninth Kid. "With that spinning head and aching waist, you had better lie down. We are leaving."

Zhou withdrew his palm from his forehead and listened to the sound of the two bandits and the donkey leaving. He leaped up abruptly.

"Lie down? Your old lady's minge hair I will!"

Scared by Zhou suddenly jumping up and screaming obscenities, Neighing Horse gawked at him. Sprout also ran out of her room to tend to her father.

"No one will talk to me. Who can I keep counsel with? I will lie down, lie down, lie, your old lady's –"

He paused because Ninth Kid had doubled back and was staring at him from the gate.

"Who are you haranguing?" Ninth Kid asked.

"Ah, ah, this lad here. I didn't want to lie down but he bugged me about it. I need to plan the tree felling and the brick making, so how can I lie down? I was thinking of taking off my shoe to slap him in the mouth."

"Oh, oh, I thought something was wrong with you. Your apprentice means well. You can still think it over while you are lying down."

Ninth Kid left. Righteous Kindness Zhou no longer bounded or cursed. He thudded down on the ground once more with his face muffled in his hands.

The shoemaker wracked his brain for a whole night but still failed to hit upon a good idea that could galvanise the villagers into discussing how to build the compound for the bandits. So, he resorted to a clumsy ruse. He told Neighing Horse to help him haul the sack of returned grain to every household to share. In passing, he told them that they needed to lumber up the mountains to cut down trees, to make clay bricks and to build a compound. "Whether you take the grain is up to you. If you refuse, I will leave a few handfuls at your gate. I don't give a damn if it's snaffled by pigs or pecked by the chickens – that is your business. My business is informing you that we need to fell trees and make clay bricks.

"Hey, Water Born! The bandits gave back a sack of grain for every household to divvy up between us. Please bring out a litre container. By the way, the bandits want to build a compound and need us to go up the mountains to cut down trees. Whether you go or not, you should make up your mind."

"Gold Nugget! The bandits want to build a compound and require us to make clay bricks. I have relayed the word to you. Whether you do it or not, you are your own master."

In this way, Righteous Kindness Zhou toured every household in the village, including Old Fourth Ren's and Steamed Bun's. When the sack was empty, the word had been relayed to every last family. Draping the empty grain bag across his shoulder, the new Village Head went back home. At the centre of the street, he halted and pondered for some time. Then he threw back his head and, screaming while slapping his chest, roared at the villagers of Ancestral Worshippers Shrine:

"Listen up, all of you! The bandits are neither my maternal uncles nor my grandpas. You know clearly how I, Righteous Kindness Zhou, became the Village Head. I have received no benefits from them. They want to build a compound. I can't do it alone. If the compound is not built, they will occupy our village. You have to think about whether the compound should be built or not. After you have thought it through, you can go up the mountains to cut down trees or make clay bricks."

After that, he went to the uplands alone with an axe. He reasoned to himself: "I have done my duty and I am felling trees. I don't dare offend the bandits. By the same score, I haven't forced anyone among you. I can only proceed in this way and the Old Lord Heaven is my judge."

The mountains were serene and only the sound of the solitary Righteous Kindness Zhou hacking away at the wood was to be heard. He gave the job his undivided attention. He shed sweat and bared his arms. It dawned on him out of the blue that cutting timber like this was the best job in the world. Trees never intimidate you. Trees never give you the cold shoulder or complain about you, let alone humiliate you. Good, cut it down, cut the son of a bitch down!

Ai, ai, ai, some had gone up the mountains with axes, saws and ropes – all tools used for felling forests. They were all strapping young labourers from Ancestral Worshippers Shrine, including Steamed Bun and Old Fourth Ren's son.

He wanted to greet them. They apparently didn't want to pay any attention to him. There was no need to exchange greetings; just put your back into it.

Now came the sounds of swishing axes, saws being worked and palms being spat upon. There was also the cracking sound of trees being tugged down with ropes. The men were dwarfed by the boundless mountains. It was as if several crickets were stridulating on an expanse of grassy marshland.

Zhou sneaked the odd glance at them. Their arms were bare now too. Their biceps bulged and their sweat glistened like greasy emulsion. Their hands and bodies were bursting with strength. But they were simultaneously afraid of the bandits and petrified of the homemade rifle. They were in the same boat as him.

He studied Steamed Bun. The young man was nineteen with an athletic frame. It was no wonder that Sprout liked him. He swung the axe resolutely and forcefully, his determination conveyed by the sound.

Axes could be used to fell trees. Why then couldn't they be used to cut down people? Oh, oh, axes were not forged for that purpose. They were different from homemade guns and long blades. Oh, oh, axes could be used to cut down people, but once terror-struck by the sight of the homemade rifle, the axe-wielders found the strength sapped from their hands and bodies.

Ka, ka, ka, ka. Another tree tumbled down.

Ninth Kid and Profound Meditation Wu were standing in front of the Heaven and Earth Temple. They could make out the woodcutters on the mountains opposite.

Enthused by the spectacle, Ninth Kid proposed: "Let's join them."

"No, no," was the old man's response.

"I am sitting on my hands here and my body and bones are suffering unbearably."

"If you feel idle to the point of discomfort, you can chop at the bricks with your blade. Think what it would mean if you joined them in this job."

Ninth Kid thought for a time and then it clicked. "Fine, I will order our men to ply their blades in the courtyard or chop at the bricks."

A little over two months later, Ninth Kid and his gang moved from the Heaven and Earth Temple to the newly-built compound. The compound included three main rooms and two rows of wing rooms as well as a kitchen and a donkey pen. The latrine stood outside.

Profound Meditation Wu named their home *Loss and Gain Compound*. To the outsiders, he declared that it meant in one's life you lose a little and gain a little. You must lose something whenever you gain something and only if you are willing to lose can you have the chance to gain. To the gang, he explained that it meant if you are prepared to lose your life, you can gain anything you want.

Ninth Kid and Profound Meditation Wu took up residence in the main chambers.

"Might we be counted as having succeeded in sitting tight here?" The former enquired of the latter.

"Almost. But we are still some distance from resting on our haunches."

"You are like a private tutor."

"The ancients advised: we should brace ourselves for danger in times of safety."

"Oh, oh, you really have become a private tutor."

The autumn crops were ripening in the fields. There was no need to leave the courtyard to inhale their heady smell. Ninth Kid admitted that he was fond of breathing in the fragrance.

"This is a dangerous sign," Wu warned.

"How so?"

"We are not farmers but bandits. Different types of folks have different kinds of noses. We shouldn't be roused by the same things."

Ninth Kid held his tongue. He was not convinced by the old man's logic. Couldn't a bandit's nose take a liking to the scent of crops? He felt that Wu was putting on airs, deliberately coming across as inscrutable and a little showy.

14.

The moment Earthen Jar stepped into the Loss and Gain Compound, he let out a wah! and then cried. He was alone with only two donkeys in tow.

All the others in the compound, including Ninth Kid and Profound Meditation Wu, sped out of their rooms. They formed a scrimmage around Earthen Jar and called out his name. He seemed to have neither seen nor heard them and only cried.

Ninth Kid was perturbed. "You son of a jackass, you have been away for months. Then when you come back, you say nothing and just blubber."

Earthen Jar wept louder and used his hand to wipe the tears from his dirty face while wailing.

"You son of a jackass, how have four donkeys become two and where is Third Matcher?" Ninth Kid demanded to know.

Earthen Jar released the donkeys' reins and used both his hands to mop his cheeks, weeping inconsolably.

"You son of a jackass, you turned back halfway without even getting to the village?"

Earthen Jar wept buckets while shaking his head hard.

"You son of a jackass," Ninth Kid snarled. "A dozen or so guys are on tenterhooks waiting for your report. If you cry again, I will sew up your mouth!"

Earthen Jar finally burst out: "My wife's run off with another man!"

"Your wife has run off. What about the other women?"

"Your wife and all the other wives are gone. The old people

and the children have left too. Not a shadow of any of them can be seen in our village. Not even a ghost remains." He got ready to squat down to bawl his eyes out.

Ninth Kid, who was truly exasperated, stopped him in his tracks. He swung his arm full stretch and slapped Earthen Jar's dirty face. His victim staggered backwards with his hand clasped over the smarting spot. Now silenced, he stared straight at Ninth Kid.

"Keep on crying!"

Seeing that another slap was likely, Earthen Jar jumped further backwards. "I won't. The moment I came into our village, I broke into sobs; I whimpered all the way back. I have almost cried my guts into rags and I have wailed enough."

"Since you have wailed enough, now you can talk."

"I have answered all your questions."

"Be more detailed."

"Fair enough. Not a soul was left in the village. All the women have gone. My wife …"

Earthen Jar was about to cry again. Realising that Ninth Kid's palm could swing over at any moment, he pleaded: "Don't. If you went back home and your wife was nowhere to be found, not one man and not even a single dog was around, you would do the same. Third Matcher and I sat in our compounds sobbing for half a day. Then we sobbed on the street for half a day. Later we moved to the village gate and cried until our eyes were swollen, and the four donkeys kicked out their hind legs. Then we doubled back."

"Where is Third Matcher?"

"Halfway back he said he couldn't carry on and insisted that he would go and search for his wife. I replied: 'The world is huge. Where can you hope to find her?' I reminded him: 'Your wife has gone off with another man. Even if you did manage to find her, she is already someone else's wife. So who the hell do you think you are? If you maintain that she is your wife, the other guy will spit on your face.' But Third Matcher didn't listen. I then said: 'I can't take care of the four donkeys together with the grain all by myself.' He replied: 'I don't want you to herd all the donkeys back.' He took two animals. If I'd refused, he would have crossed blades with me and I was no match for him."

"Where is the grain?"

"I sold it."

Earthen Jar took out a fistful of silver coins and handed them to Ninth Kid. He added: "Matcher also took half of the silver coins. If I didn't give him them, he would also have duelled with me." Earthen Jar then took out the piece of brown paper. "Our home village has gone. In every courtyard there are weeds half the height of a man. If we go back, all there is to see are the insects in the scrub."

He handed the map to Ninth Kid, saying: "Take it as a keepsake."

No one uttered a sound, including Ninth Kid.

"Fair enough, fair enough," Profound Meditation Wu broke the silence. "Nobody had been expecting that, but now everything has been made clear. Fetch some food for Earthen Jar."

"I don't want to eat anything; only to cry my eyes out."

Earthen Jar cried with abandon.

This continued for days. After he had eaten and drunk and cast aside his bowl and chopsticks, he habitually either shed tears or sat in a trance. When he sat in a trance awhile, his eyes invariably moistened.

"Earthen Jar," Wu observed. "You have cried the skies cloudy over this compound. This is a den of sighs."

"I haven't actually cried. Just shed tears."

"You have made everyone turn on the waterworks. Can't you see that?"

"I'm not to blame. Everyone has their own problems to grieve over."

"Look at you. Are you still a true man or not?"

"I behave like this exactly because I am a man. If I weren't a man, none of this would affect me."

"Can you turn off the tap, please?"

"I can't. Give me a wife, then my tears will go away naturally, without effort. My face will be all smiles."

"I can't do that for you."

"Then don't rip into me about weeping. I still have tears aplenty."

"But they won't bring you a wife."

"It's because they can't bring me a wife that I must shed tears. If they had brought me a wife, there'd be no need for you to remind me. My waterworks would already have shut down."

"Oh, oh. Then go ahead. But be careful. Ninth Kid might box your ears."

Ninth Kid didn't box Earthen Jar's ears. Instead he studied the brown paper intently. During the next few days, he frequently took out the sheet to examine it. Presently, he called over Earthen Jar.

"I don't believe that our village hasn't a soul in it now," the chief said.

"Go and see for yourself. None of the villages for several dozen square miles around has anybody in them. Our village is not alone."

"You son of a jackass, have you settled your wife somewhere?"

"*Yi! Yi!*"

"Maybe in a certain village in the vicinity?"

"Old Lord Heaven is above our heads."

"Swear you haven't hived away part of the proceeds from selling the grain?"

"I swear on the Heavens, the Earth and my conscience."

"How can you be sure your wife ran off with another man? You haven't seen anyone. So how can you know?"

"Just think about it. There wasn't any food, any drink, any hope. Now, supposing a fella were to appear and say: 'Come along with me.' She'd follow him, wouldn't she? If this wasn't the exact sequence of events, she might have hung a lock on the gate and gone away of her own accord to the *kang* of another household somewhere else."

"You said that you went to my compound to take a look. I believe you. But I could never believe that my wife would follow another man and leave."

"*Yi! Yi! Yi!* My wife, your wife, all our wives – the whole lot of them walked away. But you don't believe what I'm saying. You always cross examine me like this. You might as well have slapped me to death and that would be that. I don't want to say one more word."

"Don't bear down on Earthen Jar," Wu advised Ninth Kid. "If I were your woman, I might very well have walked off with another man too."

Ninth Kid was curious.

"She might have been willing to stay, but her stomach probably wouldn't. A man has an insect's mouth. The moment they open their jaws, food must be crammed in. Just tot up how long we've been away. To fill their empty stomachs, people might be prepared to sell their bodies and their sons and daughters. It's a law of nature – just as the skies will rain and birds fly away. Let's take a step backwards to make this point clear: Going off with some other men could be seen as a viable escape route."

"The way I see it, you should no longer be obsessed with this," Wu continued. "You miss the village, but it has become a river beach rank with wormwood; you miss your wife, but she has become another man's woman. There is no point in missing her."

"What about our kids? Our offspring have also become the kids of other guys."

"Children are different from women. A woman belongs with whoever feeds her and provides her with a *kang*. But your children are still your bones and blood even though they are at the opposite end of the horizon. Whoever feeds them is doing you a favour – nobody can change this fact. There is no point then in missing them either. Just let them grow tall; let them shoot up. In the future, if you happen to be reunited, they are your children; if you don't, they are still your children. We are all in this world. So why should you still miss them? There is no use in missing them. You are the chief."

"The way I see it," he continued. "No women, no home and no compound means that there are no ties in this world. From now on, the Loss and Gain Compound is our home. We dozen are intimate brothers. You should wrench your mind towards this fact."

Profound Meditation Wu's words worked. A few days later, Ninth Kid told him that, after wrestling with it, he had now finally succeeded in coming around to his way of thinking. What is more, he had hatched a plan. Now he needed to bring the residents of the compound to the main room to put their heads together.

"What is your plan and how have you thought it out? Let me in on it first," Profound Meditation Wu said.

But Ninth Kid didn't give an inch, promising: "You will know when it comes around."

All the bandits congregated in the main room.

Ninth Kid took out the map on brown paper and showed it round, declaring: "At my orders, Earthen Jar painstakingly scrawled away in the hope that it might one day be put to use. However, after he used it just once, it's now useless. As our village is gone and our women have decamped with other guys, it has no purpose anymore. Nobody needs to go back there. It is trash and no mistake. That being so, we don't have any ties in this world." With these words, he tore the brown paper into shreds and threw the remnants over his shoulder.

Ninth Kid went on: "When our donkey-back gang first hit the road, we were a team of twelve. Later the hare hunter joined us and we were thirteen. Now one has left and we are back to twelve. Does anyone else want to leave? If you want to leave, then please go ahead. Not only will I not prevent you, but I'll give you some money for your travels. Anyone?"

No one wanted to quit.

"The one who left us said that he went off to look for his woman. Do any of you want to look for *your woman*?"

"She is already another man's missus, but my prick is still my prick."

"That's the spirit," replied Ninth Kid. "Even if we did try to find them it would prove a wild goose chase. We won't leave here and we won't look for them. We have a shortcut. We will raise women where we are!"

"Ah, ah, ah, ah? *Raise women*?"

"Yeah, we will raise women," reiterated Ninth Kid. "My mind kept wandering here and there in the last few days and my head almost became a dried-up stump of turnip. But Profound Meditation Wu snapped me out of my confusion. He said that I was obsessed with useless things and that I should think about something practical to keep my mind occupied. He was right and I followed his advice. If Old Broke Heaven is unfair, then man should take action himself. You know that I said this to Heavenly Music Zhao."

"People are not grain," Wu reminded him. "When grain is in your hands, you can tuck in whenever you want. But that might not be the case with people."

"We will try. We will cross the river by groping at the rocks along the riverbed. We will know better after we have tried and groped. If we hadn't tried already, there would be no Loss and Gain Compound."

"We will relieve people of their wealth – yes – but never of their women. When we first hit the road, we agreed on this. You even hurled abuse at Earthen Jar because of this. Have you forgotten?"

"When we first set out, we didn't say that we would build a Loss and Gain Compound at Ancestral Worshippers Shrine. When I berated Earthen Jar, we were not entitled to say that we had enough food and drink. But we do now. When I hurled abuse at Earthen Jar, I thought our women were still there. But now I know they are not."

"If you argue like this, I can't out-argue you. But I never expected that you would wrench your mind this way."

"Raising women is more troublesome than raising grain. We can't just impose our will and have it done. If we can't raise enough women in one round, we will do it several times in different batches. We will also draw lots and wait in line. When we have succeeded in raising some women, we will allocate them according to the order. I won't draw a lot. I will put myself last in line. The hare hunter will not draw a lot either but stand at the head of the line. Why? He wields a powerful firearm."

"No, no, no," the hare hunter declined. "I don't want a woman. I have been screwed over by them in the past. You raise your own and I won't be red-eyed with jealousy."

"You son of a jackass, do you want to leave?" Ninth Kid queried.

"I don't. If I wanted to leave, I'd have done it early on. Hunting hares alone bored me stiff. I like a lively crowd."

"It is OK if you want to leave, but you should leave behind your homemade gun."

"I've no intention, no intention at all."

Profound Mediation Wu also said that he would neither draw a lot nor wait in line. He stated that sometime in the future, if they could really strike roots here as Ninth Kid had said, he would find a mistress and nibble on snacks like he had done in the past.

No one begged to differ and Ninth Kid's words were final. They drew lots.

"From now on," Ninth Kid instructed. "You guys should keep your eyes peeled and your feelers out. See whichever household has a good woman and get her registered under your name."

Earthen Jar asked if he could pick and choose. Ninth Kid said: "You can't pick and choose if that woman is already registered. However much you might want to pick and choose, you should follow the order. Those standing in front of you will choose first. Unless, that is, the woman you have in your sights is willing to follow you." Ninth Kid added that he put himself last because he wanted to look about.

"Oh, oh," exclaimed Earthen Jar.

They were soon well-acquainted with the women in the Ancestral Worshippers Shrine community. Their excitement became feverish because the number of women far exceeded demand and there were both married ones and chrysanthemum-like virgins. "This is our first step," Ninth Kid noted. "After the autumn harvest, we will take the second step."

Earthen Jar registered Sprout under his name.

"I want to slap your face!" Ninth Kid yelled.

Earthen Jar asked why.

"Sprout is the Village Head's daughter and we can't touch her. Whether we can manage the second step all depends on her father."

Earthen Jar felt dejected and muttered: "Oh, oh."

Profound Meditation Wu couldn't set his heart at ease.

"Don't be agitated," Ninth Kid consoled. "I will fix your words in my mind. I will never provoke them into being like locusts."

Profound Meditation Wu still felt uneasy.

Ninth Kid laid out his way of thinking: "Just imagine: we are not going to raise a woman from every household. We have got twenty to thirty women registered, but we will claim only nine or ten of them. Can nine or ten households whip up like a swarm of locusts? Even if they could, they'd be squashed with a single stamp."

15.

Ninth Kid handed Righteous Kindness Zhou a list of names and made his message brief and succinct: "Number one, every man at Ancestral Worshippers Shrine who ought to have a woman already has one. None of us at Loss and Gain Compound has. This is not on. Number two, the collection of grain should be of secondary importance this time. Women will be offered first and then the grain. Whichever family offers a woman will be exempt from having to hand over grain. Number three, all of the families that have an available woman have been added to the list. Now, which family should give its woman? You can either summon all the villagers to compare notes or darken their doors one by one to inform them according to the list. When a family has been talked round, a woman will be taken. Number four, your daughter's name hasn't been included on the list. But if you choose to wash your hands of this business, she will be the first one to be taken. If you don't do your best, she will be taken then too."

Righteous Kindness Zhou gawped at the ceiling like a dead fish. He grasped his ankles and froze in that position. When the Loss and Gain Compound was being built, he stood on a ladder conveying tiles that were dislodged from the roofs of the other buildings to be utilised on the bandits' compound. Someone pulled a wicked trick and hooked the ladder so it would topple over, spraining one of his ankles. For weeks, he stayed at home to recuperate. The last few days had seen him get down and shuffle about, but he was still on the *kang* most of the time. In the hope that his sprained ankle would heal quicker, he started to massage it the moment he got down from the brick bed. When Ninth Kid led the marksman and Earthen Jar to look for him, he was still in that posture. "Don't get down. Continue with your massage," Ninth Kid said. "I will leave after a quick word."

When Ninth Kid had finished his second sentence, Zhou's eyes once more took on that dead fish appearance and the hands that were gripping his ankles became like stone.

"I am through, Village Head."

No response was forthcoming.

"I am leaving."

Panic seized Righteous Kindness Zhou and he immediately took hold of Ninth Kid's arm. "No, no, no," he yelped. "Don't leave. You spun out a long string of words, but only four of them lodged in my mind. Then my brain faltered and nothing else sank in."

"Which four words?"

"*Women will be offered.*"

"Those four words are enough. The rest doesn't matter."

"It does. I heard the words that matter clearly, but I failed to understand them."

"Then should I repeat them?"

"No, no, no. First explain the 'women will be offered' bit. What do you mean by that?"

"Every bloke at Ancestral Worshippers Shrine who ought to have a woman has one already. Did you get that? None of us at Loss and Gain Compound has. Did you get that? This is not on. Therefore, women shall be offered. One woman will be offered for each of them. Now do you get it?"

"Oh, oh, it seems like I've been listening to something that was said in a dream. Is there such a thing in this world?"

"Many strange things have been seen in the world and all the things in this world are the work of man."

"Oh, oh, you said that everyone in the village who ought to have a woman has one already. That is not right. I, for one, don't have another half."

"Then one will also be offered to you. It's no inconvenience for us. Just look around. Tell me if there is anyone you have your eye on and I shall bring her to you."

"No, no, no. I didn't mean that. I meant, if we take other men's women, then they will have none. What are they to do? You at Loss and Gain Compound will be set up but at the cost of others being made single. Isn't that so?"

"Your brain swirls very nimbly. I hadn't thought that part through. Then we will collect virgin girls first and make up any shortfall. Tell them to broaden their minds a little. They have women around them every day, but nobody at the Loss and Gain Compound does. Share and share alike. We will return them on the day we leave."

"My lord, women aren't chairs. They're not benches, socks, cloth shirts."

"Try. Just try and then you will know."

"Women are not shoes either," said Zhou. "You can try on a pair of shoes to see if they fit, but this is not the case with women. I can't handle this business."

"Take a good look at the list. I said just now that your daughter Sprout is not on it."

"Sprout has an intended already. I've accepted the other party's betrothal gifts. The marriage ceremony will be held in a few days and every villager knows that. You know it too. It's my predecessor's son Steamed Bun."

"Even so, you should still be the one to handle this business. Otherwise, your Sprout will be the first to be taken away. I have just made this perfectly plain to you. Someone tried to stake a claim to Sprout already and I gave him short shrift. I asserted she is the Village Head's daughter and nobody can lay a finger on her. Why? Because he is the Village Head and will take care of it for us."

"Then find another Village Head. I am not up to the post."

"Ah, ah? Say that again."

"This post is way beyond me. I mean what I said, I mean what I said."

"Then tell your apprentice and Sprout to put your affairs in order. You decide on a date. This is also good for Sprout. After entering the Loss and Gain Compound, she won't have a tie in this world."

"No, no, no, no. When I said the post was beyond me, I meant that everybody in the village is giving me the cold shoulder. It is such a big undertaking. If no one wants to talk to me, who can I compare notes with? Do you know how my ankle was sprained? No matter who you install as Village Head, the others will snub him. If you want someone to be the Village Head, you should first of all ensure that the others are willing to cooperate."

"Oh, oh, you mean that you are prepared to try?"

"Why not. Whether it will succeed or not, we should at least try. When I said 'find another Village Head,' I didn't mean that you should kill one and replace them. If you kill one and put another in the post, then kill that one and put another in the post, you will work your way through everyone until nobody's left. If you want me to collect women for you, you should first make the villagers talk to me. I guarantee that if I say the Village Head will be changed, they will talk to me. If they talk to me, the river water is boiling hot and then I can try. This is what I mean."

"Oh, oh, you mean I should help you stage a drama for the villagers to watch," Ninth Kid probed.

"Yeah, yeah, yeah."

"What if the drama is a dud?"

"There's no chance of that. I know a thing or two about human hearts. I am also a man. Just try. Take it as a dumb-show. Have a try."

Ninth Kid laughed, admitting: "I never expected that in order to gather women I should have to pull some stunt first. Interesting, interesting. Then we will put on a drama."

"If you are going to do it," Righteous Kindness Zhou recommended. "Make it lifelike."

"I will order the marksman to butt the back of your head with his gun in full view of the villagers. Do you think that would be sufficiently lifelike? Or rifle-butt your forehead."

Righteous Kindness Zhou thought for a minute and then responded: "I'm not keen on either."

Under duress, he opted for the back of his head. "Out of sight, out of mind," being his reasoning.

He made one further request: "Can the marksman be told to keep his finger a safe distance from the trigger?"

"If his finger is even a little too far away from the trigger, it won't seem lifelike. The shooter is an old hand," he reassured. "If I don't say the word, he won't fumble his digit blindly."

"So you won't say the word?"

"I'm not interested in your death, only in seeing that the women are offered up without any hassle. As long as everything goes smoothly, I won't interfere."

So, a dramatic scene was staged.

The men of Ancestral Worshippers Shrine were again squatting in the courtyard of the village office. The homemade gun of the self-taught marksman did indeed butt into the back of Righteous Kindness Zhou's head. Ninth Kid announced: "This guy is unwilling to be your Village Head. You must swap him for another. After the new Village Head has been elected, he must bury the dead body of his predecessor. Whoever wants to be the Village Head, stand up. If nobody is willing to stand up, we will draw lots as we did last time. Whoever draws the lot is the new Village Head."

Zhou shivered. He was not putting on a show. He was genuinely terrified – not at having the homemade gun shoved into the back of his head but at the thought that someone might stand up.

Nobody did.

No one was prepared to draw a lot either.

"Since none of you has stood up or is willing to draw lots, then you must think out a way for this guy to continue being the Village Head," Ninth Kid ordered.

Righteous Kindness Zhou's legs didn't tremble so violently now. "I won't be the Village Head. I am a worthless excuse for a man. I am a traitor as far as this village is concerned. Death would be better than life for me. Hurry up and exterminate me. With one quick bang, I'll be released."

"That can't be allowed," Ninth Kid growled.

Righteous Kindness Zhou's heart was lighter now. "Since nobody will stand up and it is such a rigmarole to draw lots, I shall recommend one for you. Make quick work of me. I don't want to be the Village Head because I don't want to live."

Righteous Kindness Zhou then scanned the crowd and his eyes landed on Gold Nugget.

Gold Nugget's face altered. He knew that if Righteous

Kindness Zhou called out his name, the homemade gun would be thrust against his head. He couldn't allow Righteous Kindness Zhou to do that. "The Village Head does his job well. How can he quit?" he asked volubly. "There is no need to make a recommendation or draw lots. I suggest that the Village Head should continue doing his duty."

His words immediately drew an affirmative response from all present. "Agreed. Agreed. Agreed."

Righteous Kindness Zhou's ears seemed to have been plugged. Surveying around again, his eyes fell on Steamed Bun.

"Uncle Shoemaker, you can continue doing your duty," he answered. "All your fellow villagers are imploring you."

"Village Head, you hear that?" yelled Ninth Kid. "All your fellow villagers are imploring you. If you say that you will quit again, I will order the shooter to open fire on the spot."

Emboldened, Righteous Kindness Zhou brushed aside the rifle pointing at the back of his head and said to all present: "If you want me to continue being the Village Head, never spit at me again."

"We haven't," was the collective response. "No one has done that. We won't."

"I have sprained my ankle," explained Zhou. "Now my waist and legs are giving me gyp too."

"The Village Head is thinking too much. It won't happen, it won't happen." His neighbours were now adamant.

"Gather together all the shoes that I have made," requested the cobbler.

"Right you are," they concurred. "Whoever has placed an order ought to claim them."

"If anything occurs, we should compare notes."

"Yeah, we should compare notes carefully."

Righteous Kindness Zhou softened his voice and said that he had something he needed to discuss with them. He took out the list given to him by Ninth Kid and read out the names. "Those guys whose names are reeled off should come here tomorrow morning after breakfast. Alright?"

"Fine, fine," they answered.

How could they have conceived that they would be comparing notes on whose family members should be donated to the bandits? It was so unlikely that such a series of unexpected incidents would unfold. "Fine, fine," they promised and were very amiable towards Righteous Kindness Zhou.

Righteous Kindness Zhou appeared to be satisfied and was also warm towards Ninth Kid. "The drama definitely wasn't a dud. I knew it wouldn't be," he cackled. "Next, I will try to talk with them."

Ninth Kid felt satisfied as well. The moment he entered the Loss and Gain Compound, he told Profound Meditation Wu: "It went off very smoothly, very smoothly. The Village Head is setting the next step in motion for us."

16.

"Father," Sprout called out. "Neighing Horse overheard what went on between you and the bandits. He told me everything. Are you really going to supply women to them?"

"Yeah."

"You and the bandits have practically become family," his daughter grumbled.

He looked at Sprout. "Neighing Horse hasn't told you about the drama thing?"

"He did."

"Then you can't lecture your father like this. If I hadn't promised to raise women for them, I'd have been long dead by now and they would have already spirited you away to their lair. Your father doesn't want to become family with them. But if he had died, those overtures would have been in vain. Tell Neighing Horse to fetch Steamed Bun. I want to have a word with him. If Steamed Bun still retains a shred of a human heart, he ought to talk with me."

The lad came as requested. "Sprout," her father ordered. "Wait in your room while I shall have a word with Steamed Bun. After that, you two can talk."

"Steamed Bun, it is good of you to drop by," Zhou reflected. "You haven't spoken to me or to Sprout for months. You see how ghastly her eyes have become from all that crying? If she continues like this for even a few more days, her eyeballs will end up rotten and blind. Is your heart a thing of flesh or stone? Don't you know Sprout misses you every day?"

He continued: "Do you know why the Village Head was going to be changed? The bandits wanted to raise women from the village. You didn't see that coming? It's beyond normal human reason. By rights I should call you a brat, but whenever I address you by your name you should listen. You witnessed twice how the Village Head was elected. Shouldn't you spare a thought for your shoemaker uncle's painful guts? What am I going on about? The guts – or intestines – are linked with the heart. They know and share the pain of the heart. You gave your uncle the cold shoulder. I don't blame you. I don't blame our neighbours either. In an odd way, I ought to be grateful to them. Today, no matter who stood up in the village office and said that he was willing to be the Village Head – just imagine – your uncle would have met the same end as your father. Sprout would then have been taken away to the bandits' lair. An even more pathetic fate than your father's."

Righteous Kindness Zhou went on: "I shall address you politely by your name one more time and you must listen up. Your uncle has summoned you today with two intentions. He wants to air his grievances and he wants to talk about the business between you and Sprout. Tell your grandpa, grandma and mother about your midnight run. Don't look down upon your uncle. If you do look down upon your uncle that doesn't matter, but don't let Sprout get caught in the crossfire. Sprout is a good girl; a dutiful girl. Take her away. You might roam as far as the end of the skies and she will still be a dutiful girl. A fine match for you. You need never worry about her causing you to lose face. Get away with you – both of you. Leave Ancestral Worshippers Shrine. It will be dangerous if you don't. Let me muddle through with our neighbours and the bandits. I will persist until the bandits have left and you shouldn't come back before then. You hear me loud and clear? Your uncle is imploring you."

"Today when you stared at me, I was petrified that you might recommend me as the Village Head."

"It never crossed your uncle's mind. Nor did letting anyone else do the job. Your uncle is paving the road for you and Sprout. Go talk with her. You have her ear. Talk with her in a thoughtful way. Your uncle is waiting for your reply."

The door curtains swished aside and Sprout stepped in. "Father," she said. "Don't put Brother Steamed Bun out. I won't leave. I can't leave you behind and Brother Steamed Bun can't abandon his family."

"Brother Steamed Bun," Sprout enquired. "Do you think you could leave behind your grandpa, your grandma and your mother?"

"I don't know."

"Father, you have not given it a thought; can you and his family cope if we both leave?"

Righteous Kindness Zhou ducked his head. "I did think it through. I concluded that you must leave. If you don't leave, I must be hell-bent on gathering women for the bandits. I can't imagine what will pan out next. Steamed Bun, do you have an inkling?"

"Not a clue."

"Could you have predicted that my father would be telling you to take me away?" Sprout interjected.

"I could. When Neighing Horse instructed me to visit, that very thought struck me. I will go back home to brush my house now. For the time being, I will only think about the business between you and me."

Steamed Bun headed home, bumping into Earthen Jar en route. This took him completely off-guard.

Earthen Jar was deeply sullen. The origins of his downcast feelings could be traced back to Ninth Kid's rebuke. He was desperate to claim Sprout for himself, though the chief vetoed that. None of the other women had such an exemption. Why was the Village Head's daughter off limits? Wasn't she a lady too? Beneath her fine exterior maybe she harboured a contrary temperament. Or maybe Ninth Kid just wanted her for himself? He was anxious to bring up this topic once again, but didn't dare. A far greater ennui set in.

Today, when they went to the Village Head's home to discuss the minutiae of recruiting women, Sprout's bedchamber lingered in Earthen Jar's mind. He wanted to slip in to cast his gaze over her, but was too afraid. In the grip of his temper, Ninth Kid might snatch the homemade gun to blast off his face. It seemed inevitable that mistresses would be gathered and the exercise counted a success. Still, the woman offered to each bandit would not necessarily be their personal favourite. How could you not be gloomy? Lying under the quilt, Earthen Jar thought about this. The more he thought about it, the more sullen he felt.

When he could no longer bear his own sullenness, he went to take a piss. After emptying his bladder, he no longer wanted to burrow into his quilt. So he hung about aimlessly outside. He hung about and hung about until his aimless feet carried him to the entrance to the village. Then to the village street. He subsequently bumped into Steamed Bun, who was approaching the threshold of his compound.

Steamed Bun shouted: "Halt, halt!"

He didn't grasp his long blade in his hand. He fumbled to where it should have hung and then remembered that he had been loitering about after relieving himself. He wasn't properly kitted out.

Steamed Bun stopped in his tracks.

"It is so late," observed Earthen Jar. "Why haven't you gone to bed? Why are you drifting around?"

Finding that Earthen Jar was alone and, what is more, he wasn't armed with his long blade, Steamed Bun became a little more courageous. "I went to the Village Head's home," he answered.

"The Village Head's home? It is so late. You are not sleeping at home but went to the Village Head's home? What for?"

"He called me over. He wanted to marry his daughter off to me, but I refused."

"You refused and that is the right thing to do."

"Why?"

"The Village Head hasn't told you that women will be raised?"

"He has. But he also said that his daughter was counted out."

"Listen to him spewing rubbish. If she is not offered up this time, she will be offered up next time. It is a dead cert."

"Why?"

"Our chief has her reserved for himself. Though he hasn't said it out loud, the seed is planted in his mind."

"Oh, oh."

"I wanted to have her registered under my name, but our chief wouldn't allow it. Gloomy, so damned gloomy. I really want to tell the Village Head and request that he talk with his daughter. She's bound to end up in the Loss and Gain Compound sooner or later. Why can't she follow me? If they nod in agreement, our chief will have nothing to say. But I don't dare."

"Why?"

"What if I fail to talk them round? What if our chief gets wind of it? It would be good for her to be with me. I would be very nice to her. I was born kind to women. *Ai, ai*, I'd forgotten to ask: is his daughter willing to marry you?"

"It's not a matter of her being willing. I said no."

"How come?"

"Her father took over the post of Village Head from my father. You know that?"

"Oh, oh, a knot has been tied in your heart."

"When I said no, she cried. She is still crying now."

"It would be so nice if I were in your shoes. Both sides could agree and everything would fall into place. But I am not you. There always has to be some weird twist of fate."

"Compared with your chief, you are a better match for her. Your chief is too long in the tooth."

"It's as I've told you: in this world there always has to be some weird twist of fate."

"You don't dare try. Do you even want to try?"

"How can I?"

"I will call her out and you can confide in her."

"Can you get her to come out?"

"Sure, but I am afraid that you'll be tongue-tied."

"Out here? On the street?"

"Find another place. The Heaven and Earth Temple? You are familiar with it."

"Let me think. What if I fail? Then I am dead meat."

"She won't blame you if you can't talk her round. She will only blame me. But that doesn't perturb me."

Earthen Jar gave it his all and went to the Heaven and Earth Temple.

Steamed Bun also had to give it his all since he had been the one to set the ball in motion. He worked out that the big steelyard weight used by his family to measure out grain was the most suitable weapon. He went back home and fetched it.

Having sat waiting in the Heaven and Earth Temple for what seemed an eternity, Earthen Jar suddenly felt a little unnerved. The longer he sat, the more the feeling grew. Unable to sit tight, he stood up and strode out of the temple. When he reached the gate, he came face-to-face with Steamed Bun.

"Is she coming?"

"Of course. I wouldn't dare bullshit you."

Earthen Jar craned his neck to look into the void behind Steamed Bun.

"Don't look behind me. She is here!" He swung his arm at full stretch. The huge steelyard weight described an arc in midair and struck Earthen Jar's temple with precision.

The second strike came soon afterwards.

There was no third strike because Earthen Jar had already fallen limp. Steamed Bun pounced and gripped the bandit's throat with both hands like grim death. By the time he loosened his grip, Steamed Bun's fingers were already stiff. He knelt down before Earthen Jar panting.

Not knowing how to deal with the situation, he hauled the body to the kitchen behind the main hall of the temple, folded it up and crammed it into the stove. Earthen Jar was all floppy. Steamed Bun was scared to look anymore, but found several clay bricks and flung them in the stove again and again until the body was covered. He did all this because he was loath to look at him. Out of sight, out of mind. Earthen Jar had disappeared – gone.

Steamed Bun fled the scene. It was not until the moment he raised his feet that he realised that his legs felt brittle. His knees virtually buckled at every step.

He also felt the heaviness of the steelyard weight, which had been hooked around his little finger all along. Through every action, it had remained in situ.

He tossed the bloodied apparatus into the river.

Rather than returning home, he pushed open the gate of Sprout's compound with a bang. The moment he crossed the threshold, he collapsed, paralysed, into the arms of Neighing Horse.

When inside, he gathered everyone and recounted the story of Earthen Jar's "disappearance." Their faces all changed.

Righteous Kindness Zhou couldn't rein in his tongue. "Whi, whi, which one?"

"The one who always trailed the marksman. Earthen Jar."

"Brother Steamed Bun, you committed murder," Sprout cried out.

Neighing Horse was terrified to the point of tears and crammed his head into the quilt.

Sprout looked at her father and at Steamed Bun. "What should we do? What should we do?"

Zhou didn't say a word.

"Give me a mouthful of water," Steamed Bun said. Sprout poured a bowl for him, which he tipped down his throat in one gulp.

"What should we do, father?" shrieked Sprout.

"Steamed Bun has done nothing. Steamed Bun, do you hear me? You haven't done a thing. Even if a Heavenly King interrogates you, your answer will always be the same: I have done nothing."

Steamed Bun nodded his head without ceasing.

17.

All the men whose names were on the list crowded into the village office. There were twenty-nine of them in total.

Righteous Kindness Zhou told them they had been asked over to compare notes about the village women. They were taken aback.

"You have been summoned here to put your heads together. Why you? Because your families have unattached women and the others don't. There is no use calling them in. It is none of their business. Even if they did come, they would only take it as a chance to witness the fun. That's why they haven't been invited."

"It is not that every single family will have to offer a woman," Righteous Kindness Zhou continued. "Only nine or ten will be compelled. For that reason, we should have a pow wow. Which families are to be chosen? We must get into a huddle and reach a conclusion."

"Righteous Kindness Zhou," the village men crowed. "You really have some gall. You talk such crap, yet stay calm-faced as calm-faced can be?"

"This is a big event. It wouldn't do to grin," Zhou replied. Each man then spat at him.

He mopped his face a number of times. "We made an agreement last night that no one should spit at me."

"Yesterday we didn't know the topic for discussion. Now we do know, we can't help spitting on you," they retorted. They spat a second time.

Zhou again wiped himself clean. "If you only spit and

don't compare notes, the problem will never be solved."

"We can't debate what you've asked us to debate. You should debate with our spit." A third mouthful flew.

They left.

Righteous Kindness Zhou neither blocked them nor tidied his face. "Leave; just leave. I will report our meeting to the bandits using your phlegm as the minutes."

The moment he stepped into the Loss and Gain Compound, he shouted out: "Look! All of you come and look."

The bandits herded around him. Pointing at his face, Righteous Kindness Zhou said: "Look at this."

"Spit," Ninth Kid laughed.

"They each spat at me three times. The first two volleys I wiped clean. What you can see is the last one. This is the result of me trying to reason with them."

"Hurry, wipe it off and try again," rasped Ninth Kid. "Tell them that one woman less is needed now. One of our number did a midnight flit."

"Oh, oh."

"That son of a jackass had Sprout in his sights. I wanted to slap him across the chops. He went off in a huff. Good riddance. He has deserted and relieved your burden one notch."

"Since we have got the ball rolling," Zhou responded, "it doesn't matter whether one more or one less has to be offered. The problem lies in that they only spit and never put their heads together. If I go over there again, more phlegm will fly."

"What are we to do then? If we handle matters ourselves, your village will be cast into chaos."

"If you pick off one or two first they will be more willing to get into a huddle. That won't cause any chaos."

"That's a good idea. Whoever spat on you first, we will go to his home to fetch his woman."

"There were twenty-nine of them but I vaguely remember it was Gold Nugget."

Ninth Kid asked how Gold Nugget's woman was.

"Delightful," Righteous Kindness Zhou replied. "She has curving eyebrows and big eyes."

"Then we will pay him a visit."

A clutch of bandits busted down Gold Nugget's gate. The moment the homemade gun was rammed against his forehead, he dropped to his knees with a thud and rolled his eyes upwards.

"Gold Nugget," Righteous Kindness Zhou pronounced. "Don't do that with your eyes. It is not your life but your wife that they want."

Gold Nugget's raised chin twitched a few times but his eyeballs still swivelled so that he didn't witness the manner of his spouse's departure.

The strange movements ceased and he shut his eyes tight.

The Village Head stood firm. "Gold Nugget," he said. "You can look now. They have gone away. Lend me your ear. Now you know something of the ache I've been having in my guts and can tune into my pain. Help me gather everyone to discuss this. Should we find a way to choose an extra woman, yours can perhaps win her freedom."

Gold Nugget slapped his own face. "OK, I will follow you."

Gold Nugget had a spring in his stride. When he reached each home, he threatened: "Come along or not. If you don't, the bandits will pay a call and bust down your gate. I will show them where you live."

The twenty-nine villagers soon assembled in the village office once more.

Righteous Kindness Zhou started proceedings. "One fewer woman is needed because one of the thugs went AWOL last night."

"Why don't all of them go away?" the others grumbled in chorus. "Go away, all of them!"

Gold Nugget interrupted them: "This is farting nonsense. Get down to the real nitty gritty." They did so in earnest.

Someone suggested that they should first of all single out those women who were obnoxious to the elderly and fond of quarrelling with their husbands and making a scene, as well as those who were bratty and frequently threw tantrums in front of their parents. But nobody admitted that his wife was such a woman and likewise there were supposedly no delinquent daughters. Every wife was apparently dutiful and every daughter a docile girl. Those who had previously complained to the contrary all changed their tunes. They maintained that all their past words had been merely tossed about and none was grounded in fact.

Another proposed that since all were good women and girls, they should draw lots and leave it at the disposal of the Heavens and luck. Again, nobody was willing to draw lots. Even the proposer refused.

They discussed awhile and *ahh*-ed awhile, *ahh*-ed awhile and discussed awhile, bemoaning that it was so exhausting, but still they failed to strike upon a promising method. Gold Nugget was on a knife edge. "Wrack your brains," he pressed. "My wife is already in the bandits' den. You mustn't be so selfish and only look after yourselves."

"Then let the Village Head have the final say," the company concluded.

Righteous Kindness Zhou didn't participate in their deliberations. "It is your business and your decision is final.

I won't air my opinion," he declared. "I don't want to live my life with saliva dripping from my face every day."

"Skip the spittle part," they said. "You are still our Village Head and whatever you say, goes."

"But the Village Head doesn't want to offend anyone. My position is far more thankless than yours. You only have the bandits to be scared of. I have both them and you to contend with."

Someone patted his head and crowed: "*Ai, ai*, this is a village matter and the Village Head can't wash his hands of it."

Another immediately echoed: "Yeah, why isn't Sprout's name on the list? She shouldn't be exempt. The Village Head can't accept favouritism. Everyone should be treated equally."

"Sprout has been promised to Steamed Bun," Zhou rejoindered. "They will be wed properly in a few days."

The others then ran rabid.

"Our women have given birth to babies, but your Sprout hasn't even moved into her husband's household," they protested.

"Since Sprout has been promised to Steamed Bun, Steamed Bun has a woman now," someone said. "So why hasn't he come to talk it over?"

"Yeah," Gold Nugget agreed. "I will rustle him up."

"Fine, go ahead," Righteous Kindness Zhou consented. "If Steamed Bun agrees to put Sprout on the list, I will have nothing to say."

Steamed Bun was brought over, but would not permit Sprout to be included.

The men were furious. "Our women will become the bandits' playthings, while you tie the knot with Sprout? That mustn't be allowed. Sprout is not your woman yet. How can you be part of the quota? Shoot!"

Steamed Bun was taken aback and his face became red and swollen. "I killed a bandit!" he blurted out. "One fewer of them means one woman will be saved. That's why I'm owed that quota."

"Ah, ah, ah," began Righteous Kindness Zhou, keen to keep up the pretence. "One bandit did go missing. But he quit of his own devices. How can you say you killed him? What rubbish are you churning out?"

"It isn't rubbish. If you don't believe me, you can go to the Heaven and Earth Temple to take a look. In the kitchen built by the bandits. Inside the stove."

The others held their tongues and stared fixedly at Steamed Bun.

"If you are up to it, you can claim a scalp too and free up a quota for yourself. Are you man enough?"

"I don't believe him," someone mocked. "Where did you find the balls?"

"What the hell do you care where I found the balls? Balls or no balls, I did him in!"

"Fine, fine, OK, you killed him, you killed him. Keep your voice down," the others replied. "How did you do it?"

"I whacked him with a steelyard weight."

"That's strange, strange," they mulled. "A steelyard weight, the Heaven and Earth Temple, the bandit. It's unbelievable."

Steamed Bun then told them how exactly he had turned the measuring implement into a lethal weapon.

Now they seemed placated.

"Do you dare do the same?" the murderer asked.

No one uttered a sound – including Righteous Kindness Zhou.

"Why didn't we think of that?" said Gold Nugget eventually. "We outnumber them three to one. That's not even counting the other villagers. Why didn't we think of this?"

"If you do start to think this way, I shall leave and have no part in it," the Village Head stated. "You can talk it over amongst yourselves."

"Don't worry," reassured Gold Nugget. "I was just saying. I don't know whether it will work or not. I was just saying."

One neighbour asked Steamed Bun: "Did you think you were capable of taking a life before this?"

"I don't know. I bumped into him and struck out in a moment of confusion. My legs are still like rubber now."

It was true. The bandit had been alone, with neither a blade nor a firearm to hand. Anyone could have lashed out at him without fear of retaliation. But even if the villagers thronged forward together and were prepared to fight the bandits to the death, one of them would still need to head the charge. The leader would be at the mercy of the rifle and all the blades. Even if all the bandits were decimated, he would most likely be forced to forsake his own life. He would not savour the following days alongside the survivors.

They were at a stalemate. The bandits were given the latitude to select the women themselves. Originally, nine or ten women were required. With one bandit dead and Gold Nugget's woman gone already that left two down and seven or eight to go. There was no need to talk it over again. No matter which woman was to be taken away, the man of the house would be left to suffer alone. True, only a minority of the village men would suffer but each one hoped they would not be among that number.

They all clung to this hope as they dispersed.

"Don't breathe a word of what Steamed Bun has done to anyone else," his future father-in-law insisted. "One bandit less, one more thorn dug from our flesh."

18.

"Righto, righto," Ninth Kid said. "You have had your chitchat and we now need to do our part. We will collect the women early tomorrow morning."

"No matter which family you go to it will be the same story as Gold Nugget's," surmised Righteous Kindness Zhou. "I can guarantee it."

"Fine, fine. After that, we will be done with it once and for all. You can come to the Loss and Gain Compound to share some wine at the wedding banquet."

The moment he stepped into his home, Righteous Kindness Zhou admitted to Sprout: "I'm almost scared to death. Steamed Bun has told the others what he did."

"Did he really or are you pulling my leg?" Sprout wailed. "How could he go shooting his mouth off? How could he?"

"Don't fret. Nothing bad will happen to him. The bandits will raise the women tomorrow and after that everything will be fine. The bandits won't know a thing."

"No, no. Fire can't be wrapped in paper. The bandits will get wind of it sooner or later. Neighing Horse, fetch Brother Steamed Bun."

Before Neighing Horse could do so, Steamed Bun had come of his own accord.

"I felt regret," Steamed Bun said. "The moment I blurted it out, I regretted it. Now the more I think about it, the more scared I am. I can't sit tight at home. What should I do?"

"Father, did you hear that? What should we do? What should we do?"

Righteous Kindness Zhou replied that the bandits would not know.

"But just in case!" Sprout persisted.

"There is no *just in case*. After the women are raised, the bandits will become restive."

"I want to take Sprout to a place of refuge," Steamed Bun told her father. "You promised to let her leave with me."

"I am worried about Sprout, but the situation has changed and soon I won't worry any longer. After we have toughed it out tomorrow, the trouble will be over."

When the next day finally dawned, Righteous Kindness Zhou awoke early and set about his business. He didn't go out but sat in the courtyard listening to the movements in the village. Soon, a bout of crying and shouting was to be heard. After a short interval, the shouting began again. "Listen," he said to Neighing Horse and Sprout. "The bandits are raising the women. Hurry, hurry," he prayed. "Old Lord Heaven, please make it happen quickly. Let them get on with it. Once it's over, everything will fall into place."

Unexpectedly, Ninth Kid suddenly pushed the gate open and entered. Neighing Horse and Sprout slunk to their respective rooms.

The patriarch got ready to stand up.

"Sit down, sit down. I will sit down too," Ninth Kid said. He unsheathed his long blade and planted himself cross-legged opposite Zhou with the weapon on his lap. The bandit leader was all smiles.

"You have raised enough women?"

"No, it is a very hard nut to crack. We dragged, yanked and carried, but they kicked, shouted and cried – very forcefully, in fact. If several of us tried to tackle one, we'd all end up drenched in sweat. But you were right; the men were all submissive like Gold Nugget. The moment they spotted the homemade gun, they caved in. They rolled their eyes but didn't say a thing."

"We are all only human."

"I have also found a woman for myself."

"Good, good, from which family?"

"You will find out soon."

"Water Born's wife?"

"No, no. Wait a while."

Righteous Kindness Zhou stood up. He saw the marksman approaching with his homemade gun butting at Steamed Bun. "What's up? What's up?" Righteous Kindness Zhou asked. He stared at Ninth Kid.

"I thought that my man had run away at midnight. After much ado, I found out that he'd been killed by Steamed Bun. Someone grassed him up. At first, I couldn't believe it. But finally I went to the Heaven and Earth Temple and dug what was left of him out of the kitchen stove."

"Steamed Bun, what's wrong with you?" thundered Zhou. "You have killed someone?"

"Brother Steamed Bun," Sprout cried, dashing out of her room with the intention of running to her betrothed. Ninth Kid blocked her with his long blade. "Sister, don't be so rash," he warned. "Once the shooter hooks his finger back, your Brother Steamed Bun will be history. Hurry on back to your room so you won't get caught in the crossfire."

Neighing Horse bustled Sprout back to her room.

"Steamed Bun, you have killed someone?" Zhou shouted at the accused.

Steamed Bun stayed quiet.

"Village Head, stop playing possum," his opposite number snarled. "My man was killed by him. I brought him here to compare stories with you. Do you still want to give Sprout to him? Tell me if he should live or die. If he dies, what would Sprout do?"

"Don't order someone else's death; never do that. We will continue to raise women but nobody must lose their life."

"To let him live is unconscionable. It would mean my man died in vain. How else should I avenge my dead brother? Chop off one of his arms? Or a leg? Are you willing to let Sprout marry a man who is missing a limb?"

"No, no."

"Then I will put my cards on the table. Originally, I did not consider taking away your Sprout. But now I've changed my mind. Surely, it is no big deal to let him go? You just said: we can continue to raise women but nobody must lose their life. Steamed Bun must hand over Sprout and find another girl."

"No, no. Sprout is my daughter. By what rights can he hand her over?"

"She is your daughter, but she is also his betrothed."

"Sprout will not marry him. Is that good enough?"

"Then let him die."

Sprout flung aside Neighing Horse's hands and dashed out of her room. "Father, you can't let Brother Steamed Bun die. I am his bride. If he dies, I will follow suit!"

"Village Head, did you hear that?"

"Sprout, go back to your room. Your father is begging you. Right?"

Neighing Horse again shuffled Sprout back to her chamber.

The old man's eyes were already glistening: "I have done my best for you. I have done my best for you and you can't break your promise. You promised you wouldn't take Sprout. You can't go back on your word. I have done my damnedest. You should leave me a way out."

"Your words sound twisted. So, you have a way out if Sprout follows Steamed Bun but you don't if Sprout follows me?"

"You can't tear something away with brute force. A melon wrenched off its vine won't taste sweet."

"Those words sound even more warped. All the other women have been wrenched off their own vines. Why else would we be forced to drag and carry them, and why would they kick, cry and shout? You said that a melon wrenched off by force won't taste as sweet. This is wrong. As long as it is a ripe melon, it is always sweet whether it is picked gently or roughly. A woman is not a melon."

"Why can't she be with Steamed Bun? They both consent. Ah, *ai*!"

"I told you: he has killed my man. If he doesn't die, doesn't lose an arm or a leg, then he must lose his woman. Die or turn over Sprout," the bandit cawed to his captive. "Which do you prefer?"

"I don't want to die. But I won't turn over Sprout either."

"Your words don't count."

"Sprout won't follow you."

"Her words don't count either."

Righteous Kindness Zhou dropped to his knees and slapped the ground: "Heavenly principles get thrown away! Ah!"

"Village Head, don't be like this. Tears can't bring back heavenly principles. There are no heavenly principles in this world, only human principles. I will take his woman away."

"No! No! Sprout is not his woman. Put me to death but don't spoil Sprout. Steamed Bun, see what you have done? You have screwed over your beloved."

"It was me who killed your man," the boy confessed to

Ninth Kid. "Do away with me."

"That is a different kettle of fish. Whether you live or die, Sprout is going with me."

"Kill me. Let me die!" Zhou interposed, suddenly springing to his feet and dashing his head against the wall. His skull was on the point of being cracked against the brickwork again when a mob led by Water Born swung into the courtyard.

Ninth Kid tensed himself and extended the long blade in his hands.

Water Born darted towards Righteous Kindness Zhou and restrained him by taking hold of his collar. His face was livid with indignation. He barked: "You shouldn't have to die. Whatever happens, Sprout should first be sent to the bandits' den."

Ninth Kid felt a little calmer.

Someone flung a brick at Righteous Kindness Zhou's window.

Taking hold of the Village Head, Water Born again flashed at Ninth Kid angrily: "They are all women. Why is this guy's daughter not being taken away?"

Another brick was pelted at the window.

"Wasn't I right?" the bandit asked Zhou. "There are no heavenly principles only human principles. I have to take Sprout away. Whether I want to or not is irrelevant. You are the Village Head. You should set a good example. The other households will be easy to handle then." Turning to Steamed Bun he observed: "I am leaving you with a way to save your skin."

"You had better kill me," the prisoner said.

"I will go to the bandits' den," Sprout said calmly to their aggressor. "There is no need to drag or yank."

"It is the Loss and Gain Compound, sister," Ninth Kid corrected her.

Water Born let go of Righteous Kindness Zhou.

"Leave. My word is my bond," Sprout said.

Water Born and his vigilantes left without a sound.

"What great good fortune and enviable karma you must have to meet a lady like this," Ninth Kid observed to Steamed Bun. "Mark her words and don't hate the guy who squealed. He blabbed because he wanted to claw something back – he wanted me to let his woman go. I don't reward people who stoop so low."

He again said to Sprout: "Sister, don't be afraid. I will let you live a good life. I and the Village Head will be waiting for you in the Loss and Gain Compound."

The marksman turned his rifle in the direction of Righteous Kindness Zhou. "Put it away, put it away," Ninth Kid said. "Let the Village Head walk ahead of us."

They filed out through the gate.

Stuttering out "why, why, why?", Neighing Horse wanted to say something but failed. He then sang: "*Yi, ah, ai*, why, *ah, ma*, has it come to this?"

"Neighing Horse, you can mooch around on the street as long as you shut the gate behind you," Sprout said.

Only she and Steamed Bun were now left in the courtyard.

"Brother Steamed Bun," she said.

He ducked his head and avoided eye contact.

"Brother Steamed Bun, neither of us will die," Sprout reassured. "So let's wear a smile on our faces." She became her usual self again and escorted him to her room, whispering, "There's something I want to show you."

Sprout opened her carved wooden box and took out a number of colourful garments as well as a pair of embroidered shoes. Sitting on the brick bed, she held one item after another against her body for her fiancé to appreciate. "These are all parts of my dowry that I've made myself. Every day, I long for you to marry me. On our wedding day, I will let you watch as I put them on one by one. Look, look, aren't they pretty?"

Steamed Bun didn't dare to notice.

"Brother Steamed Bun, I sent them on their way because I wanted you to see this. Otherwise, I wouldn't have allowed them to take away my father without me."

Steamed Bun now paid her close attention and turned his gaze on the vibrant wardrobe she had squirreled away. Sprout slipped on her embroidered shoes for his private viewing. "Sprout," Steamed Bun beseeched. "Don't show me this. I don't even want to live. I have screwed you over."

Sprout seemed to have heard nothing. She unclasped another small wooden casket at the head of the brick bed and took out a pair of intricately stitched sachets. "Brother Steamed Bun, I made these for you. Even my father felt jealous. Originally, I had wanted to give them to you on our wedding night. Take them. They were made for you, so they are yours to take." He declined, so she stuffed them into his pocket.

The paramour took hold of his beloved's hands and gazed intently at her face, which was now bathed in a smile.

"You will really follow the bandits?"

"Yeah."

"You would do this for me?"

"I am doing this of my own free will. Bandits are men too. They shouldn't be without a woman."

"For your father's sake?"

"Brother, I know that you hate my father. Don't take that attitude. Ah?"

Tears flowed out of Steamed Bun's eyes. He gripped her hands tighter, seething: "I won't allow you to follow the bandits."

Sprout retrieved her hands from his grip. Steamed Bun muffled his face with his fingers to hide the coursing droplets. His sobs suggested a knife was gashing his heart. He then wailed piteously and tried to staunch the flow by slapping his own cheeks.

Sprout took hold of Steamed Bun's hands. "Brother Steamed Bun, don't. I won't allow you to cry. I want to show you more."

Sprout undid her buttons one by one. "I wanted to preserve it and not show you until our wedding night. But that day will never come. I told Neighing Horse to go out so that now you can feast your eyes."

Sprout started to undress. She even took off her red bodice. Conveying not a hint of shyness, she disrobed herself entirely.

"Brother Steamed Bun, how do you want to watch? You can watch in any way you like."

"Sprout!"

Steamed Bun's face paled as if he was feverish.

Sprout grinned unperturbed. She ushered Steamed Bun's hands to her breasts. His fingers were very stiff; not at all how they used to be.

The young woman lay down, dropping her tender body onto the wedding garments.

"Sprout," whispered Steamed Bun.

And still, her face beamed. "Brother Steamed Bun, I will lie down here for you. After you have had your fill, it will be time for me to hand myself over to the bandits."

"Sprout …"

His whole visage seemed to be contracting, becoming uglier and uglier.

"Brother Steamed Bun, do you want me? If you want me, I will give you …"

Suddenly, Steamed Bun cried at the top of his voice and darted out.

Sprout duly handed herself in at the Loss and Gain Compound.

19.

Ninth Kid wanted to stage a collective marriage ceremony with drums beaten and flags flapping. "That would draw too much attention and need too much effort," Profound Meditation Wu warned. "We had better be cautious. It is still hard to say if you can really be spliced together because this is not a proper legal marriage where matchmakers have been used."

Ninth Kid heeded his advice.

"Then we will shut the gate and pair up. After that, we will retire to our brick beds. The hare hunter will stand vigil at the gate, sacrificing himself for the night. Those inside won't be allowed to go out and those outside won't be allowed in. Give them some time to pleasure themselves and then they will be satisfied. If you don't believe me, just wait and see."

There were nine women in total. Eight men made their selection according to the order decided upon by the lots drawn beforehand. Sprout was chosen by Ninth Kid and nobody grumbled.

Ninth Kid said to Profound Meditation Wu: "Aren't you red-eyed with jealousy?"

"I am not that way inclined. But I'll still seize the opportunity for a nibble when the need arises," Profound Meditation Wu continued. "Anyhow, you are blessed. Among the nine women only yours is a chrysanthemum-like virgin; still so tender."

They were one room short. "Had we known beforehand," Ninth Kid admitted, "we would have built an extra space."

"It doesn't matter," said the old widower. "I shall share with the hare hunter and that will do."

"That is what I'd hoped to propose. After a few days, we'll add another bedchamber."

It was not until later that the bandits knew that on that night none of the eight cuckolds at Ancestral Worshippers Shrine slept on their brick beds at home. A carpet of needles must have been spread out on them – invisible and irretrievable bodkins that prickled so persistently that sleep would never come. Instead, the men were just outside the village spying on the Loss and Gain Compound. Gazing at the compound, they imagined how their women were fooling about with the bandits on their brick beds. They were not in one single location but scattered across eight different spots. How could they unite as one front?

Steamed Bun found it impossible to sleep too. After running out of Sprout's home, he stopped crying. He ran out of the village. He observed Sprout from afar as she stalked over to the Loss and Gain Compound. His heart missed a beat as if a pebble had been dropped down into a well. He moved to several different places, crouching down on a field ridge, then sitting in an earthen trench with his head leaning against the sides. His hand pinched at the constituent clods without stopping, scrunching many into powder. His mind now wandered to Sprout's tone when she called him "Brother Steamed Bun" and then to her body as she was lying on the bridal dresses. His mind wandered and wandered until he began thinking of how the bandit Ninth Kid must now be pressing down on her frame. He couldn't imagine how Sprout would cope. He didn't want his train of thought to turn this way, but his mind couldn't help probing there.

Sprout always addressed him as "Brother Steamed Bun". Would she be doing that beneath Ninth Kid? Would she gleefully call out "Brother Steamed Bun"? His mind then strayed to the homemade gun. *Bang*, his father's face had been blasted off; obliterated. That gun could remove anyone's face. In the past, it had been crammed into his mouth and jabbed against his forehead. *Bang*. It would also go off at him with a *bang*. "Brother Steamed Bun," Sprout's voice rang out in his head. She was being pressed down upon by the body of the bandit Ninth Kid. Steamed Bun moved again, squatted down and became entangled in his thoughts. He then moved to another place, but could not escape his all-encompassing thoughts. His heart seemed to have been seasoned with fiery chilli powder. He neither hunkered down nor sat tight but started to loiter aimlessly. He loitered and loitered all the way to the Loss and Gain Compound.

A lantern was hanging at the gate of the compound.

The self-taught marksman rose from the stone pillion and aimed the homemade gun at Steamed Bun.

"Get lost!" he shouted.

"It's Steamed Bun."

"I told you to get lost."

Steamed Bun thrust out his empty hands. "I can't fall asleep, I am at a loose end."

"Find another place. You can't make yourself fall asleep by being at a loose end. I feel sleepy but am not allowed to go to sleep. I can't hang about. Who else is with you?"

"I am alone."

"Do you have any tobacco?"

"Yeah."

"Toss it over."

Steamed Bun threw the tobacco pouch at the sentry's feet.

"Good. Now, get lost. I will roll a fag for myself."

"I want to smoke one too. If you are alright with that, please return the pouch to me when you're done. The papers are in there too."

"Stand still and don't move."

"I won't move. Not an inch."

The marksman started to roll his own; his weapon within handy reach.

"Your lass has followed Ninth Kid."

"She is not my lass. Her father has always been wary of giving us his blessing."

"Women are like water, they flow along wherever their hearts lead them."

"I wouldn't know."

"How old are you? Don't you have any experience? After you have got some experience, you will know. Women are like flowers too. They float away on a gust of wind. I've had my moments with women and what is more I've been screwed over by them. You'll still be none the wiser for me telling you. Nor will they. Raise women? Suit yourselves, but I won't. I am standing guard for them here."

The marksman threw the tobacco pouch back to Steamed Bun.

"You roll yours," the guardsman told him, standing up to light his fag from the lantern flame.

Steamed Bun bent down to retrieve the tobacco from the ground. He arched like a cat and, without warning, surged towards the self-taught marksman with a whoosh and snatched up the homemade gun. The marksman had barely taken a single drag from his roll-up when he turned around to find the homemade gun pointing directly at his nose.

"Freeze," Steamed Bun yelled.

"Brother …"

"Shush."

"Oh, shush yourself."

"Which room is Sprout in?"

"The main room on the left."

"Do you want to live or die?"

"To live."

"Then sling your hook. Get as far away as possible."

"Alright, alright. You will never see me again in this life."

"Pick up the pouch and treat yourself to a smoke on the road."

The marksman gathered the tobacco and flexed his legs to run away.

With the rifle in his hands, Steamed Bun headed directly into Ninth Kid's room. The door had been left carelessly unbolted. The chamber was illuminated brightly by a few candles. Ninth Kid was perched on top of Sprout and had fallen fast asleep. Steamed Bun jabbed him hard on the back of the head with his firearm. The bandit leader sat up and turned to look at Steamed Bun with one hand stroking the spot where he had been lunged at so painfully. He seemed not to have fully woken up yet.

Sprout was roused too. She fixed Steamed Bun with her eyes wide open, clearly wanting to push aside the man who was riding on her body.

"Freeze," Steamed Bun roared.

Sprout obeyed.

Ninth Kid, who was startled fully awake, gasped: "How did you get in?"

Bang! All the gunpowder and iron shot was discharged into Ninth Kid's face. He slumped over. Sprout let out a shriek, sat up and grasped a piece of clothing to cover her modesty.

The rest of the bandits were startled awake. They all sat up straight on their brick beds.

Steamed Bun stood at the gate: "Listen up, all of you. Ninth Kid is dead. I have killed him. Stay where you are and don't try anything. Anyone who dares to move, I'll make his head burst open like a flower."

No one stirred. They were all surprisingly passive.

The only one who was not cowed was Water Born's wife. She raced out of the room without a stitch on, shrieking: "Murder! Murder!"

Crying and shouting shrilly, she made it out of the gate, vanishing to who-knows-where.

Everything fell neatly into place. The eight wronged men who were staring at the Loss and Gain Compound from eight different vantage points snatched up whatever brick or stone was to hand and dashed down. When they arrived, the eight naked bandits were already kneeling in a line in the courtyard. Their women had flung on their clothes and each brandished a long blade. The bricks and stones in the men's hands were redundant. But they didn't cast them aside.

"There's another one!" Steamed Bun yelled.

Profound Meditation Wu stepped out of the main room in spic and span clothing.

Steamed Bun butted the homemade gun at Wu's forehead.

"There is no powder in it," the old man guffawed.

When the trigger was pulled nothing was expelled. He had forgotten to refill it.

"Let us go free. We will never come back again. We will go back to our home village to farm," promised Wu.

"To farm?" hawed Steamed Bun.

"We are all peasants just like you. When we became bandits, we picked up the blades and that toy in your hands to bluff people. We bluffed our way here and succeeded in bluffing you to do our bidding."

Steamed Bun's hands were shaky all of a sudden and he couldn't grip the firearm steady. His voice also shivered. "But you have screwed people over, screwed the humanity out of people."

"That's not true. If you are human to start with, you will still be human no matter how much you've been screwed over. Just think about it."

Gold Nugget barked out: "Your old lady has released a stinking dog's fart." He brained Profound Meditation Wu's temple with a brick.

As the bandits knelt in the courtyard and begged for mercy in chorus, they were picked off without care and the men recovered their women.

Each one got a donkey too.

Steamed Bun didn't raise his hand. Sitting on the steps, he felt lifeless.

Sprout charged out of the main hall towards her lover and called out: "Brother Steamed Bun!"

He appeared at first not to have heard her then shook his head once.

"You blasted his face to buggery," she whimpered.

Steamed Bun didn't respond.

"Brother Steamed Bun, do you still want me?"

He gawped at the ground.

"Brother Steamed Bun, you don't want me?"

He raised his head to look at Sprout, drinking in her countenance long and hard.

"Go back home to see your father."

He added: "Now your father will be spared death and agony too."

Sprout stood still, apparently not grasping his meaning.

His vitality suddenly regained, Steamed Bun stood up, reached for the homemade gun and spat a mouthful of saliva on it: "*Pooh!*"

He raised a knee and smashed the firearm across it with the intention of snapping the barrel. This failed, so he slung it over his shoulder instead, then grinned at Sprout and said: "This village is no longer the place for me. I'll have no shortage of women where I'm going."

Steamed Bun strode off.

Sprout gazed at his retreating figure. She stood in the gate of the Loss and Gain Compound. Above her head was the lantern the self-taught marksman had used to light his roll-up. Nobody really knows what happened after this. What is known is that life burgeoned with ever greater prosperity at Ancestral Worshippers Shrine. Many, many years later it was upgraded into a county seat. The Heaven and Earth Temple found itself renovated into the City God Temple.

And so the cycle of urbanisation began in earnest.

Acknowledgements

The Hour of the Locust was translated by He Longping (Changsha Normal University) and Robin Gilbank (Northwest University), with the assistance of Professor Hu Zongfeng. The author and translators wish to thank Jamie McGarry and Valley Press for bringing this project to fruition, as well as Jo Haywood and J. Graham Jones for assistance with the proofreading. Financial support was provided by the China Writers Association.